Montgomery County Mills

Cover painting of Thomas Mill, Brookeville, MD
Watercolor dated September 22, 1896, courtesy of Mrs. Sylvia Nash.
Cover design by Vivian Eicke.

Montgomery County Mills

A Field Guide

by

Michael Dwyer

Copyright ©2012 by Michael Dwyer
ISBN: 978-0-578-11270-1

Published by the Mid-Potomac Chapter of the Archeological Society of Maryland, Inc.

Printed in the United States of America
Signature Book Printing, www.sbpbooks.com

Library of Congress Catalog Card Number 2012949546

For general information contact the Mid-Potomac Chapter at www.asmmidpotomac.org

*To James Sorensen, Heather Bouslog,
and all the Friends of Montgomery County Archaeology*

Contents

List of Illustrations	vii
Acknowledgments	xiii
Preface	1
Introduction	3
Background	5
Great Seneca Creek	11
Little Seneca Creek and tributaries	19
Rock Creek	23
Patuxent River	31
Hawlings River	37
Paint Branch	43
Northwest Branch	53
Cabin John Creek	59
Watts Branch	65
Muddy Branch	69
Bennett and Little Bennett Creeks	73
Little Monocacy River	77
Little Falls Branch	83
Sligo Creek	85
Notes	87
Alphabetical Index to Mills	95

List of Illustrations

1865 Map of Montgomery County, Maryland	xv
Section Through Mill Building with Equipment	1
1900s photograph of Muncaster's Mill showing the flume and the water wheel	6
Watersheds, streams and mills in Montgomery County, Maryland	9
Maryland Journal, and Baltimore Advertiser, 1783	11
Tschiffely Mill at Seneca	12
Tschiffely Mill interior	12
Black Rock Mill	13
Clopper Mill in a historic photograph from Montgomery County Historical Society, and in a 1974 photograph by author	14
Frederick-Town Herald, 1807	14
Frederick-Town Herald, February 8, 1813	15
1908 plat of Watkin's Mill	16
The ruins of Davis Mill and its miller's house in 1974	16
1910 plat for change to Hoyle's Mill Road	19
1811 notice of John Viers' intent to sell his farm and his sawmill	20
Clean Drinking on Rock Creek	23
Blair Mill	24
1880s Map of Garrett Park showing the site of Newport Mill	24

List of Illustrations (continued)

The "Old Duvall Mansion" at Newport Mill	25
Veirs Mill	25
Horner's Mill Ruins in 1974	26
1772 announcement of the sale of Elgar's Mill	27
1930s photograph of Muncaster's Mill	27
1828 notice offering mill services at Robertson's (later Muncaster's) Mill	28
Muncaster's Saw Mill	29
Bowie Mill	29
Rawlings Mill House in 1974	31
Notice of sale of Rawlings Mill	31
1879 Hopkins' Atlas, showing the southern portion of the Patuxent River Valley in Montgomery County	32
1879 Hopkins' Atlas, showing the northern portion of the Patuxent River Valley in Montgomery County	33
Lea-Haviland Mill	34
Tridelphia in the 1930s	34
From "Religious Telescope," published in Dayton, Ohio, on August 23, 1911	35
The miller's house at the site of the old Mullinix Mill in 1973	36
Notice that James Brooke will carry on Ship's biscuit bakery trade	37

List of Illustrations (continued)

James Brooke's notice to sell his gristmill on the Patuxent	37
Hopkins' Atlas, 1879, showing Brookeville with mills at both ends of town	38
Thomas' Mill, Brookeville	39
Newlin's Mill, Brookeville	39
1820s for-rent notice for the Thomas/McCormick/Weer/Hipsley Mill	39
Greenwood Mill	40
The miller's house in Speck family photograph (left) and a 1930s photograph of Greenwood (right)	40
1832 announcement that the Brookeville Woollen Factory is to be sold	41
Lucretia Harper	43
Thomas Fawcett's 1831 announcement of wool production on Paint Branch	43
The etching "Old Mill on Paint Branch" by Charles Volkmar	44
1880s plat of Dr. DuVall's Paint Branch lands showing mill property	45
1868 plat of Fawcett's Mill	47
1773 advertisement for Valley Mill	48
1783 advertisement for Valley Mill	48
Valley Mill, with the miller's house in the background, as they appeared in the 1930s	49

List of Illustrations (continued)

Miller's house at Valley Mill during archaeological investigation of the mill, 1985	49
Handbill announcing the sale of Valley Mill in 1886	51
Charles Cheney's 1783 notice to sell his mill	53
Burnt Mills on Northwest Branch in 1914	54
Burnt Mills in the 1930s	54
Detailed description of Beall's Mill property in 1784 for-sale notice	55
c. 1880 plat showing two mills on Northwest Branch	56
1930s photograph of the old site of Kemp's Mill	57
Notice of White's Mill on Captain John's Run for sale in 1769	59
August 7, 1822 notice of sale of Cabbin John Mills	60
Late nineteenth century photograph of Bell's Mills	62
Photograph of Locust Grove Mansion, 1975	63
Early twentieth century plat of Bell's Mills	64
Glen Mill	65
1926 plat of Glen Mill	66
Wooton's Mill on Watts Branch	67
1824 announcement that Perry's Old Mill is for sale	68
September 19, 1783, notice of a gristmill on Muddy Branch to be sold	69

List of Illustrations (continued)

1818 notice of Lackland's Mills for sale	70
1878 plat of DuFief's Glenwood Mills	71
1975 photograph of former site of DuFief's Mill on Turkey Foot Road	72
1832 advertisement announcing the sale of the Reverend Jimmy Day's mill property in Browningsville	73
Hyattstown Mill on Little Bennett	74
Gladhill family making apple butter at the mill in 1949	74
King's Mill in King's Valley	75
1802 advertisement for sale of Morton's Mills on the "New Wheat Road" at the mouth of the Monocacy	78
1832 advertisement for same property then known as Oakland Mills	79
1797 plat of the lands of Joseph Harris, showing the large mill pond and the smaller pond for Lyles' Mill on a stream incorrectly labeled "Seneca"	80
1844 advertisement for the sale of Lyles' Mill	81
"Remains of Old Mill on the Potomac"	83
John Eicholtz's painting, "Ruins of Loughborough Mill"	84
Location of Sligo Mill superimposed on map of Takoma Park	85
Sligo Mill's millrace can be seen running parallel to Sligo Creek in this undated photograph	85
Ruins of Sligo Mill	86

ACKNOWLEDGMENTS

The search for documents and images for this work proved to be daunting. Even when I began to collect information on the county mills almost forty years ago, there were few persons living who could recall details of operating mills in Montgomery County, Maryland. Interviews with William Dove and Charles Russell Murphy, the last of the millers at Muncaster's and Hyattstown respectively, are to be treasured, and everyone with an interest in the state's mills is indebted to John W. "Jack" McGrain of Towson, for the pioneering work that has earned him the title of "Maryland's foremost molonoligist."

Many other individuals and organizations have made significant contributions and they are (in alphabetical order): Pat Anderson, Marguerite Appleby, John Baines, Bernardine Gladhill Beall, Leonard Becraft, Heather Bouslog, Margaret Case Cahoon, Joanna Church, Doris Cobb, Arthur Colburn, Eleanor Cook, Friends of Sligo Creek, Kyle Friis, Mary Kay Harper, Bruce Hendrickson, Elizabeth Hickey, Frank Ierardi, Leslie C. King, Catherine Crawford Lavoie, Col. E. Brook Lee, Debbie Malone, the McEwan family, Harold W. Mullinix, Sr., Sylvia Nash, Debbie Rankin, Edith Ray Saul, Terry Sirk, James Sorensen, the Speck family, Hazel Lechlider Staley, Jane Sween, Robert Truax, the Veirs family, and Mark Walston.

Special thanks are due Irwin and Gloria Billick for their steadfast support, and to Vivian Eicke, Jean Goertner, Don Housley, Dorothy Krass, and Pete Peltier for their superior editing skills.

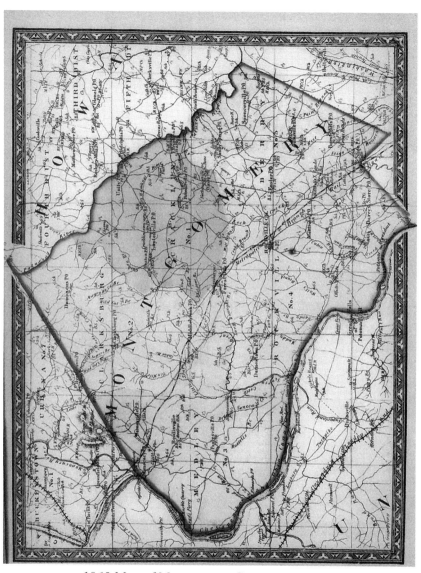

1865 Map of Montgomery County, Maryland
(Simon J. Martenet, Baltimore)

MONTGOMERY COUNTY MILLS

PREFACE

Looking at Montgomery County today, it is difficult to imagine that a time existed when its streams were the source of power that fueled technology. Man and nature have combined to erase most evidence of these rural industries. As a result, the author wishes to share over thirty years of information, acquired during his career as historian for the county's park system, in the hope that it will perpetuate interest in and appreciation for our rich community heritage.

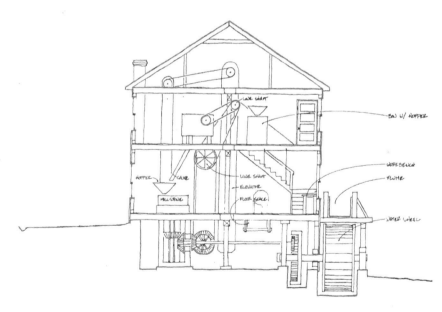

Section Through Mill Building with Equipment

(Hyattstown Mill Feasibility Study, Quinn Evans Architects, 1990)

1

INTRODUCTION

The conversion of raw materials to some form of usable product was the basis for survival in the agricultural economy that characterized Montgomery County for almost two hundred years. Grain, for example, was converted to flour and meal, trees to lumber, and wool to cloth. Primitive home chores were gradually replaced by small-scale rural industries designed to relieve or hasten the arduous or time-consuming work involved. One need only reflect on the advice offered in the *Maryland Gazette* in 1746 to "those who lived too remote from fulling mills," which were used to clean and fluff greasy wools shorn from sheep each spring.

This was but one step in the months-long process recalled in 1916 by William E. Muncaster, who added that "few persons of the present day can form any idea of the amount of work both mistress and maid of that day did on this product of the farm."

> Those people may easily thicken their cloth without much trouble or any expense. The way is when the cloth comes from the weavers to wet it well with stale urine, warmed and put it into a trough and trample it a considerable time with bare feet, turning the cloth often.[1] *(Maryland Gazette)*

"The farm," ironically, is the Magruder property that stood adjacent to today's busy Montgomery Mall shopping center, which offers ready-to-wear fashions.

BACKGROUND

Although bounded by the Potomac and Patuxent Rivers, Montgomery County's location above the head of navigation originally impeded settlement as tobacco planters had to haul their product overland to the ports of Georgetown and Bladensburg. With the increasing population and shift to the growing of grain, however, some entrepreneurs and speculators began to capitalize on the county's abundant tumbling streams, erecting mills or offering their mill seats for sale. A mill seat was a site that contained the necessary topographic elements to build a mill, namely an area that could be dammed to create a mill pond or supply of water and the hillside trench or race that could be dug (usually by slave labor) to channel the flow of water to spill over the mill wheel and release it back to the main stream. As the wheel rotated, it operated gears that turned the millstones that ground the grain. Each site was somewhat unique, and the early mills tended to be primitive. By the end of the eighteenth century, however, most mills embraced the improved technology advocated by young millwright Oliver Evans, and Baltimore grew to be the primary market destination for the booming wheat trade.

The most basic type of mill was the "gristmill," which ground grain to produce flour and corn meal and kept a "toll" or percentage of the crop as payment in a cash-poor economy. Most of the gristmills operated on this basis, which became known as "country-custom," whereas the larger mills that ground wheat for flour to be sold for export came to be known as "merchant mills." Gristmills also ground a variety of seeds to produce products like oils for use in medicines and paints; and later, ground feed for animals and substances like plaster for fertilizer. They were usually accompanied by an open-sided sawmill, which sat on a high stone foundation, enabling it to operate saws to convert trees to lumber. Blacksmith, wheelwright and cooper shops were also often associated with mill operations.

Tan yards were also occasionally located on village streams, like those at Brookeville and Hyattstown, and used tree bark and sumac leaves to convert hides into leather. Even animal bones were ground at bone mills to produce fertilizer. As one might imagine, the odors from these rendering processes filled and offended the olfactory senses. There were also a number of fulling and woolen mills. These businesses were a necessary

Background

step in reducing the home-based labor associated with the conversion of wool to usable cloth. Gradually the home carding of wool was replaced by the manufacturing process available at some gristmills equipped with carding machines, where wire brushes, attached to rollers, untangled and straightened the coarse fibers. A skilled fuller could clean, dye and full wool to make blankets and "servants' clothing" needed to dress slaves each year. During the War of 1812, these operations increased as a result of the United States' embargo on British-imported goods.

The technology required to operate all of these mills changed very slowly throughout most of the nineteenth century. Circular saws replaced the old up and down blades at the sawmills, and turbines or tub wheels proved more efficient than the old water wheel—which itself was updated from wood to metal. By the end of the century, however, the old water mills

1900s photograph of Muncaster's Mill showing the flume and the water wheel
(Early American Architecture, Library of Congress)

were on the decline as a result of advances in technology, including the use of steam, gasoline and electric power. Modern roller machinery replaced the primitive millstones, and the grain market shifted to the huge modern mills located adjacent to railways in the Midwest. For the most part, the old water-powered mills of Montgomery County had finally ground to a halt. By the 1930s, most of these abandoned mills had disappeared from the scene. Victims of decay, highway construction or arson, a few like **Muncaster Mill** (*see page 6*) and **Valley Mill** (*see page 49*) were photographed by the Department of Interior's Depression-era "Historic American Building Survey (HABS)." But most were salvaged for their materials, the machinery often going to wartime scrap drives.

Today only a handful of visible remnants are present, mostly along streams in our park system. If one wishes to visit these picturesque remnants, it is best to avoid the warmer months when foliage obscures their features. An up-county tour should include the rebuilt frame mill at Hyattstown in Little Bennett Regional Park, **Black Rock Mill** on Black Rock Road, **Clopper Mill** at Clopper Road in Seneca State Park, as well as the old stonecutting mill at Seneca State Park at the mouth of Great Seneca Creek. Down-county sites worth visiting are **Valley Mill**, in Paint Branch Park near Colesville, and the **Loughborough Mill** site adjacent to the Capital Crescent Trail in Little Falls Park in Bethesda. A series of interpretive markers has been placed at a number of mill sites in recent years in order to call attention to their remains.

Please note that it is against the law to dig or otherwise disturb these locations, and mills on private property are off limits to visitors.

Each watershed, however, seems to have its own undiscovered "mystery" mill site, and hikers are encouraged to seek these out when they are located on parkland.

In this guide, Montgomery County's watersheds are listed in order of their relative size and fall-power, which was a measure of their suitability for milling purposes; the total available water-power for Seneca Creek and its tributaries was estimated to be 1,100 feet.[1] The order of occurrence of the mills generally begins at the mouth of the stream and ascends to its headwaters until the supply of water is insufficient to power a mill.

Background
As the owners and operators of these mills changed hands many times over the years, the most recognized names—in bold in the text—are used in order to ease their identification for the reader. For example, "**Muncaster's**" mill is used instead of "Elgar's," although the latter name can also be traced in the accompanying index of mills *(beginning on page 95)*.

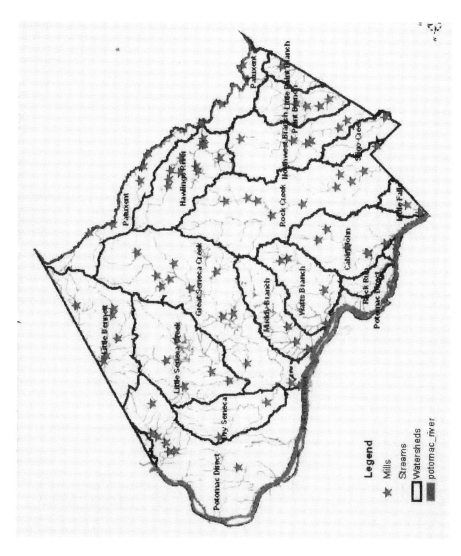

Watersheds, streams and mills in Montgomery County, Maryland
(Irwin Billick)

GREAT SENECA CREEK

Any discussion of mills and milling in Montgomery County must begin with Great Seneca Creek and its numerous tributaries, which drain almost one-third of the county. Near the junction of the Potomac River and Old River Road at Seneca was one of the largest and most enduring mills in the region. From the earliest settlement this location was perceived as an important shipping and receiving point in the quest for a Potomac trade route to the West, first by river boats, and later by canals designed to skirt the river's rocky shallows.

Few locales could inspire the breathless enthusiasm of speculators like John Ballendine, whose lengthy ad in the *Maryland Gazette* in 1769 extolled the opportunities for commerce at Seneca Falls.[1] An ad taken out a decade later by prominent Georgetown businessmen Charles Beatty, Bernard O'Neill and William Deakins, Jr., noted that their mill at the mouth of Seneca Creek was "believed to be equal to any in the state . . . bateau that will carry 15 tons, may at present come from Shenandoah Falls to the mill door . . . and that it consequently will always command considerable trade from Frederick and Washington Counties, also from Virginia."[2]

The ad noted that the mill was formerly known by the name of Eltinge's Mill. Cornelius Eltinge had come from the Hudson Valley of

Maryland Journal, and Baltimore Advertiser, 1783

New York to take up lands here in the 1730s and '40s, and a Maryland Chancery Court case details rents and repairs to his "**Seneca Mills**" throughout the 1750s, '60s and '70s.[3] By the time O'Neill and Deakins announced the dissolution of their partnership in 1783, the mill was described as "old"; but the optimism remained, however, the ad now claiming access to Fort Cumberland, 150 miles distant as well as a "favorable country custom, commanding a thick settled and very fertile country (including the Sugar Lands)."[4] George Washington also noted the supposed fertility of the "Sugar Lands" while scouting the area for the Potowmack Canal in 1785.[5]

Tschiffely Mill at Seneca
(Thomas Hahn Collection)

Over the years many investors maintained an interest in the mill at Seneca, which was rebuilt or remodeled several times. For example, in 1799 it was noted that it had been running "not quite five years" and that it was now called Millford Mills.[6] By 1855, it had become the property of John and Upton Darby, who rebuilt the mill twice before selling it to the Tschiffely family in 1902. The mill was abandoned about 1930 and torn down to make way for the new bridge at River Road in 1959. The race can be seen along the bank of the creek at Poole's Store.

Tschiffely Mill interior
(Montgomery County Historical Society)

Tschiffely Mill Road, across the street from the store, leads to the ruins of the old **Seneca Stone Mill**, on public land, which supplied the distinctive red sandstone used to build the Smithsonian Castle, among other structures. Operated in the nineteenth century, it powered its machinery using water purchased from the adjacent Chesapeake and Ohio Canal (C & O).

Upstream was the **mill of Charles Gassaway** of Pleasant Hills plantation near Darnestown, who in 1813 advertised for a "miller with a small family" to run his grist and sawmill.[7] At his death in 1816, Gassaway willed to his son Thomas "land purchased of Thomas Plater . . . with mill thereon . . . ." Plater had sold the one-acre mill seat described as being on "Hooker's Branch" to Gassaway in 1810. Plater had previously obtained parts of "Mitchells Range" from Edward Gaither,who in turn described a millrace on this tract in his will of 1777. In 1775, Gassaway's father-in-law, Ninian Beall, was selling land containing "two mill seats on Great Seneca Creek."[8] Gassaway had his lands, including "Mitchells Range," resurveyed as "Pleasant Hills." In 1820, his son Charles was assessed for a gristmill on 40½ acres of "Pleasant Hills and Thomas Discovery Fortified." A sale ad included in a Chancery Court case in the 1820s mentions "40½ acres with a large mill house erected on a never failing stream . . . good opportunity for the manufacture of cloth."[9] Apparently unable to compete with nearby gristmills at Seneca and Black Rock, it was last described in 1831 as "adjoining the lands of Major George Peter (of Montanverde) measuring 30' x 35' . . . [which] can be altered to suit a factory of any kind, there being none within 12 to 14 miles."[10]

Continuing on Black Rock Road is **Black Rock Mill**, which was built in 1815 by Thomas Hilleary, as the date-stone clearly indicates. These picturesque stone ruins were preserved as a county Bicentennial project and sit in Seneca Creek State Park where an unusual stone headrace can be seen across the road from the mill.

Black Rock Mill
(Montgomery County Historical Society)

Clopper Mill in a historic photograph from the Montgomery County Historical Society and in a 1974 photograph by the author

The next mill of significance on Great Seneca Creek is **Cloppers' Mill**, the ruins of which are also located in Seneca Creek State Park along busy Clopper Road near Germantown. A brick and stone structure was described in 1807 as the property of Zachariah McCubbin, which had replaced Benson's eighteenth century mill. It featured French "Burrs" and "Cullen's" millstones for grinding both wheat and "country custom."[11]

In 1812, the mills became part of the Woodlands estate established by Francis Cassatt Clopper of Philadelphia. The property later included mechanized wool carding. The Clopper family included famed artist, Mary Cassatt, and son-in-law, William Rich Hutton, a noted engineer who designed St. Rose of Lima Church across the street. An

To be Sold.

THE subscriber, having been appointed trustee for that purpose, offers for sale, that valuable tract or parcel of land, late the property of Zachariah McKuben, situated and lying in Montgomery county, and containing about 488 acres of land more or less. Its improvements are a large and convenient dwelling house, with all other necessary buildings, large apple and peach orchards of good fruit; also a mill house 3C by 42 feet, three stories high, one of which is stone, and the others brick, with two water wheels, three pair of stones, two of French burrs one of Collen's, with merchant and country bolting cloths, sufficient for manufacturing flour, all in good repair. Also a saw mill, stables, smith shop, dwelling house and store house. This mill stands on the public road leading from the Mouth of Manocosy to the city of Washington, about 11 miles from the former and 20 from the latter, and 20 from Frederick-town, and has the command of a good wheat country. The above property will be sold in lots or together as will be most convenient to the purchasers—the terms, of sale will be cash. If not sold at private sale before the twenty ninth day of October next, it will then be offered at public sale, on the premises, if fair if not the next fair day.
HENRY HOWARD, *Trustee.*
June 13.

Frederick-Town Herald, 1807

interesting Orphans' Court document dated 1813 apprenticed fifteen-year-old Singleton Murphy to Francis Clopper to "learn the art, trade and mistery *(sic)* of the milling business," warning the young man to "avoid card, dice . . . nor contract matrimony during said term."[12]

At the point where the Great Road from Georgetown to Frederick (present-day Route 355) crosses Great Seneca, stood the **Middlebrook Mills** complex. Originally built in 1795 by Abraham Faw, this mill was owned by a number of prominent individuals; these include Revolutionary War General James McCubbin Lingan, who was killed by a mob in Baltimore for his opposition to the War of 1812, and John Tayloe of the Virginia family that lived at the Octagon House in Washington. Now a county park, the site was last occupied by Beahms Auto junkyard; the berm constructed to prevent runoff from the business is easily mistaken for the old millrace.

PUBLIC SALE.

In pursuance of an order from the orphans court of Montgomery county, Mary land, the subscriber will offer at public sale on Tuesday the 23d of February next, if fair, if not the next fair day, at Middlebrook Mills, the residence of the late Gen, James M. Lingan, all the personal property of the said deceased, consisting of a number of valuable SLAVES, amongst whom are a good blacksmith, carpenter, cooper, house-painter and glazier, shoemaker, two good waggoners, and an apprentice to the milling business ; also, several house servants, boys and girls ; Household Furniture of every description, a Waggon and Geers, Plantation Utensils, two Copper Stills ; blacksmith's, cooper's and joiner's tools, a stock of Horses, Black Cattle, Sheep, Hogs &c.—A credit of nine months will be given on all sums over five dollars—all under that sum, cash; the purchasers giving notes, with two good securities, bearing interest from the day of sale.—Sale to commence at nine o'clock, and continue from day to day until all is sold—and the whole to be sold without reserve.

JANET LINGAN, Adm'x.

Be it known, that I have appointed HENRY WAURING and ROBERT P. MAGRUDER of Montgomery County, my attornies in fact, who will attend the above sale, and settle the business of the estate. All persons concerned will please to take notice thereof.

JANET LINGAN.

February 1 , 9t

Frederick-Town Herald, February 8, 1813

A Frederick newspaper of 1816 advertised a tract of land "two miles above Mr. Peck's (Middlebrook) Mills where a mill was for thirty or forty years."[13] This was the mill of Adin Gray on 'Grays Neck' that had been described as "indifferent" in 1783.[14] Later the site of **Watkin's Mill**, the mill seat is clearly discernable today although split by Watkins Mill Road between the race on the west and the dam site on the east. Once owned by Remus Snyder, the three-story frame mill was still standing in 1906, but eventually evolved into a radio-broadcasting site. It is now part of Great Seneca Stream Valley Park adjacent to Montgomery Village.[15]

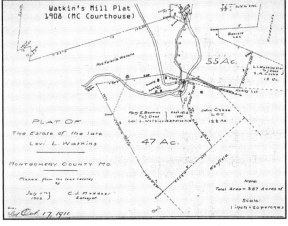

Also located near Montgomery Village is **Walker's Mill**, located on Whetstone Run, which flows into Great Seneca. This mill was built in 1877 by Nathan J. Walker, whose family had come from Browningsville. The mill is privately owned and not accessible to the public.[16]

1908 plat of Watkin's Mill
(Montgomery County Courthouse)

The ruins of Davis Mill and its miller's house in 1974
(Photograph by the author)

Another mill on a tributary of Seneca was **Goshen Mill**, which appeared on Griffiths's map of 1794 as Crows Mill. It was built along the new "wheat road" from the mouth of Monocacy to Baltimore. It is difficult to imagine how tiny Goshen Branch could have powered so imposing an enterprise as a "large brick merchant mill with two water wheels."[17] Last known as Riggs Mill before it burned in 1890, the site today is merely an indentation in the hillside on private land at the bend in Brink Road, below the "Fertile Meadows" house that features doorsteps made of the old millstones.

West of Goshen at Huntmaster and Davis Mill roads, is the site of **Davis Mill** on the main branch of Great Seneca Creek. Part of the plantation of Col. Charles Greenbury Griffith in the late eighteenth century, **Davis Mill** became the property of Dr. Washington Waters, who subsequently sold it to a miller, John Davis, who had previously worked at Goshen Mill. Built of frame, the stone foundation was stabilized in recent years as part of the Seneca Greenway project, and the millrace is clearly visible as one travels upstream along Davis Mill Road, in Great Seneca Stream Valley Park.

Deep in a wooded glen just below Butler's Orchard on the bank of Wildcat Branch, is an old stone foundation that marks the possible location of **Ford's Mill** shown on Abert's Canal Map of 1838. William Ford offered his grist and sawmill on Seneca adjacent to Major Greenbury Griffith, for rent in 1828 and for sale in 1831.[18]

Ford had obtained his land from John Magruder, who had received three hundred acres from his father, Edward. In 1800, Edward Magruder announced that he had just erected a fulling mill on Seneca near Clarksburg. Subsequent ads reveal that a fuller was wanted; and, in 1811, that Mr. Greenbury Wilson was employed as a fuller and dyer. The Magruder family continued to operate a sawmill at this location for many years, but the closing of the old road has concealed its location from view. The site remains on private property below the old Magruder homestead.[19]

The last mill along Great Seneca was **Darby's Oakland Mill**, located on private land above a broad flood plain near Woodfield. It is worth noting that the Darby family had operated mills at both the beginning and the end of this creek, among others. Described in 1941 as out of operation by 1900, it was apparently a small "powered" mill used to grind corn for local farmers.[20]

LITTLE SENECA CREEK AND TRIBUTARIES

Across the county to the west are a number of other mill sites associated with the Seneca watershed. Near Germantown in Black Hill Regional Park are the stone foundations of **Waters' Mill**. This location is reached by a steep path that runs off the park entrance road, past the site of a sensational murder in 1920, in which one of the Waters' tenant families was dynamited in their cabin. Located on the original "William and Mary" tract on Little Seneca Creek, the mill was present when Zachariah Waters willed it to his son, Tilghman, in 1819, with the provision that he would charge minimal rates to his brother for sawing and grinding. The mill was also described as an "oil" mill, most likely meaning that it was grinding flax seed, which was grown in this era. By 1895 the mill was still in the hands of the Waters family, who described it as a "grist mill that could be repaired at little expense to do a large and thriving business...."[1] It was doubtful that anyone took the above claim seriously, however, as the old water-powered mills were fading from the scene because of changes in technology and marketing. For example, the old **Hoyle's Mill** upstream was facing problems. Like his father and grandfather before him, John Hoyle was a miller who had been successful in the trade. Despite the presence of modern turbine power,

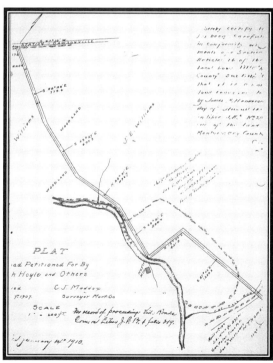

1910 plat for change to Hoyle's Mill Road (Montgomery County Courthouse)

19

the swampy, remote location on Little Seneca was doomed when the railroad came through in the 1870s. Then in 1903, the new 6-ton engine was swept away in a flood.

Smith Hoyle petitioned for road improvements in 1907. Eventually he moved his business adjacent to the railroad tracks at Boyds, where the building remains to this day. The remains of the old mill can be found by careful searching west of Hoyle's Mill Road in the recently acquired Hoyles Mill Conservation Park.[2]

> **Land for sale.**
>
> THE subscriber will sell the plantation whereon he now lives, containing 228 acres, lying on the mouth of Bucklodge, near the great road leading from Georgetown to the mouth of Monocacy, about 26 miles from the former and nine from the latter. The improvements are a good frame dwelling house with two good rooms below and two above, two fire places, a cellar and kitchen; a good large barn with a passage 20 feet square with a plank floor for the purpose of thrashing, and stables at each end, a frame tobacco house and all other convenient out houses; two apple orchards and fruit trees of other kinds. There is also a good saw mill, about 18 or 20 acres of good meadow land of which there is about 9 or 10 acres now in grass, and a sufficiency of woodland lying around the place to support it. This place is in good repair and the quality of the land equal to any in the neighbourhood, and I believe that the soil would suit the clover and plaister equal to any other land in the county. If said land should suit any person so as to purchase it, the terms will be one half down and the residue in two annual payments. An indisputable title will be given if sold and possession may be had next fall with liberty for preparing land for seeding.
> JOHN VIERS, Sen.
> Montgomery County, March 2.

1811 notice of John Viers' intent to sell his farm and his sawmill (Frederick-Town Herald)

Also located on parkland near the confluence of Little Seneca and Bucklodge Branch, near the model airpark field off Schaeffer Road, are the remnants of **Viers Saw Mill**, dating from the early 1800s. In 1811, as a result of his desire to move out of the county because of a prolonged agricultural depression, owner John Viers offered it for sale along with his nearby Susanna Farm plantation.[3]

Upstream on private property is the race of **Darby's Mill at Bucklodge**, where the Darbys, Whites and Jennings had operated a mill on the "Wolf's Cow" tract as early as the 1770s.[4]

On yet another tributary of Little Seneca was **Pyle's Mill** at Ten Mile Creek and Old Baltimore Road, near a picturesque but risky ford. As with Goshen Mill, it is difficult to believe that this was once the location of an elaborate enterprise built along a supposedly busy road, which linked the wheat-growing interior of the state with the grain port of Baltimore. The tract name "Lost Breeches" should have been a warning to original owner, Ignatius Davis, who tried to sell his new mill in 1799, later describing it as "on the new cut road to Baltimore."[5] The size of the mill's operation was greatly reduced by the late nineteenth century; a swampy clump of trees marks the location of the tailrace in Black Hill Regional Park today.

The final significant branch of this watershed is Dry Seneca Creek, located in the western portion of the county in a beautiful agricultural area. North of Sugarland Road, on private land, was the site of **Dawson's Mill**, a small grist and sawmill operated by a family that settled here in the eighteenth century.

The last mill upstream, called **Milford Mill,** was located outside of the town of Poolesville. Samuel Milford was a native of Ireland. An 1849 visit to his mill by the Medley District Agricultural Society noted that the operation was "in good order for both sawing and grinding."[6] Complaining that there were few mills to serve the area, local farmers later petitioned for a road to the mill. The mill was destroyed by fire on January 14, 1896. Traces of the road, race and pond can be found south of Jerusalem Road.

On Broad Run at Edwards Ferry Road and Club Hollow Road, stood **Young's Mill**, which, in addition to the usual services, also ground plaster, a popular fertilizer in this area during the nineteenth century. Privately owned, the miller's house remains at this location.

ROCK CREEK

Perhaps the best-known watershed in the county, because of its popularity as parkland, Rock Creek flows south from its headwaters near Laytonsville to the Potomac River at Georgetown. Georgetown was a busy seaport in the eighteenth and nineteenth centuries, first for tobacco and later for grain.

Mills lined the banks of Rock Creek during these eras. Today, the restored Pierce Mill is a reminder of these mills and is open to the public in the District of Columbia at Park Road and Beach Drive.

Moving north from the District, Beach Drive parallels Rock Creek and soon becomes Jones Mill Road in Montgomery County. The **Jones Mill** was part of the 600-acre "Clean Drinking" plantation and was described as "old" in 1783.[1] Charles Jones borrowed money from the famous Carroll Family of nearby Forest Glen in the 1800s; the loan was secured by a "22 acre mill seat on which the grist and saw mill belonging to Charles Jones stands."[2]

Clean Drinking on Rock Creek
(Photograph courtesy of Mrs. Earl Moulder)

The Jones estate was gradually reduced in size due to a number of legal judgments, including one by millwright Oliver Evans for patent infringement. Caldwell's map of 1915 identifies the site of the mill, now part of Rock Creek Park below the beltway.[3]

Northeast of there, in downtown Silver Spring, is the site of **Blair Mill**, which was fed by a tributary of Rock Creek. This was a small mill operated on the Blair family farm, "Silver Spring," which gave the community its name. The waters that fed the famous spring also powered the mill, which featured a metal wheel and was listed in an 1848 insurance

23

Blair Mill
(Library of Congress)

policy by the Mutual Insurance Company of Silver Spring.[4] The millstones remain in Acorn Park at East-West Highway and Blair Mill Road.

Two other mills not operated on a large scale were also located on small tributaries of Rock Creek near Kensington. One was **Ray's Mill,** shown on the Hopkins' map of 1879 as part of Alfred Ray's Highlands Farm that stood above present-day Kensington Parkway.[5] A millstone was returned to the town in recent years.[6] The second small mill was owned by the Wheatley family; the public road to the mill, opened in 1882, went to the property of Postmaster George Plyer on Georgia Avenue and is known today as **Plyer's Mill** Road.[7]

An interesting document in the 1870s noted that the road to "Old **Newport Mills**…had been vacated for more than forty years

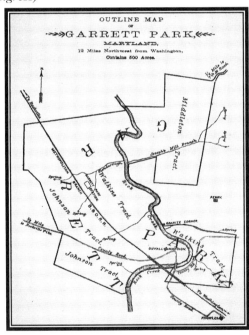

1880s Map of Garrett Park showing the site of Newport Mill
(Town of Garrett Park, 1974)

*The "Old Duvall Mansion" at Newport Mill
(Montgomery County Historical Society)*

and is now grown up."[8] Located on the main branch of Rock Creek between present-day Kensington and Garrett Park, this mill was established in 1774 by Thomas Johns and Thomas Richardson, two prominent Georgetown businessmen.[9] It provided grain for the troops during the Revolutionary War. Later, this mill was the scene of a religious service during which Josiah Henson, an enslaved worker on the Isaac Riley farm on Old Georgetown Road (in what is now North Bethesda), was converted. Henson served as the model for the central subject in Harriet Beecher Stowe's *Uncle Tom's Cabin*. Newport Mill, described as a large, stone-merchant mill, was apparently impacted by the coming of the railroad in the 1870s. Today the site is known as Ken-Gar Palisades Park, located where the Baltimore and Ohio arch crosses Beach Drive. A historical marker notes the site.

Upstream of this location was **Veirs Mill**, sometimes known as Rock Creek Mills. A two-story frame structure built in 1838 by Samuel Clark Veirs of nearby "Meadow Hall," the mill reportedly stood as late as 1927 before the improvements to Veirs Mill Road erased the site.[10]

*Veirs Mill
(Montgomery County Historical Society)*

Rock Creek

Needwood Mill, located at present-day Avery Road, began before the Revolution as a partnership between William Williams and William Dent. The latter offered his half-share of the mill for sale or lease in 1772. In 1781, Barbara Williams offered the staggering sum of four thousand dollars as a reward for a runaway "white mulatto slave named Leonard," who was a carpenter and may have worked at the mill, as his "lip and chin were split by the sawing at the whip-saw . . . ."[11] By 1800, the mill was out of repair; court testimony revealed that "there is now on the place an old decayed mill house which is worth little and which is in a situation as not to work for about two years." Regardless, the heirs of former owner Charles Beckwith maintained that it was "one of the best mills seats in the County."[12]

Horner's Mill Ruins in 1974
(Photograph by author)

Evidently a string of Rockville businessmen, including John Lodge, Adam Robb, John Braddock and Benjamin Forrest, agreed with the latter opinion, because they all subsequently became owners of the mill. By the 1840s, however, Forrest's heirs were again selling "the tract the mill was on, the race and dam still workable."[13] Eventually the property wound up in the hands of the Horner family, who operated a grist and sawmill during the late 1800s. Reportedly the mill was shut down by 1890; the wheel pit and races remain east and west of Avery Road in Rock Creek Park.

Montgomery College students conducted an archaeological dig at the Horner's (now Needwood) Mill in 1975.[14]

Rock Creek

> October 1, 1772.
> To be sold at publick Vendue, on the 20th of November next,
>
> A PLANTATION confisting of about 200 Acres of good Land, with a Merchant-Mill, and Saw-Mill on the Premises situate on Rock-Creek, in Frederick County, about 16 Miles from George-Town, 15 from Bladensburg, and 33 from Baltimore: On said Land is a comfortable Dwelling-House, several Out-Houses, and a good Orchard, about 60 Acres of Upland cleared, some Meadow, more may be made, and watered. The Merchant-Mill is Three Stories high, Two of Stone and One of Frame; the Water Wheel 20 Feet high, over-shot, with Two Pair of Stones, both double geered, fixed on a good Stream, well situate for Merchant and Country Work, in a peaceable Neighbourhood, which must be an Inducement to the Purchaser; they are esteemed well constructed Mills, &c.
> 6w
> JOSEPH ELGAR.

1772 announcement of the sale of Elgar's Mill
(Maryland Gazette)

Just east of the Needwood Mill site, the North Branch of Rock Creek joins the main branch. Several mills were situated on the north branch near the Muncaster Mill Road crossing. The first documented mill at this location was Elgar's Mill, constructed by Joseph Elgar under a writ of *ad quod damnun* in 1763, which encouraged the building of mills by allowing damages to be paid for inundating land with a mill pond. Described in 1772 as a merchant and sawmill, it was built of stone and featured a 20-foot high water wheel.[15]

The Robertson family bought the mills and adjoining "Milton" plantation and by 1820 they had constructed a new frame mill, which they rented out.[16] The Robertson's relatives, the Muncasters, assumed the property, and **Muncaster's Mill** became a local landmark with its distinctive gambrel roof. It ceased operation in 1925 and was included in the Historic American Building Survey (HABS) before burning in the 1930s.

1930s photograph of Muncaster's Mill
(Library of Congress HABS)

Rock Creek

> ## To the Public
>
> Having been employed to manage and superintend the Grist Mill, Saw Mill, and Carding Machines of William Robertson, on Rock Creek, the public are informed generally, that every attention will be promptly given in our line of business.—Having good Burr Stones and Bolting Cloth, we are making preparation to receive crops of wheat from the farmers, to be manufactured, and I think we will be safe in saying our flour, if the wheat is clean and good, will do us credit in any market. Corn, Corn Meal, Wheat flour, Buckwheat flour, Rye Chop, &c. are kept constantly for sale.
>
> The Carding and Sawing will be promptly attended to at the same time. The price for carding common wool will be 6¼ cents per lb.—Merino 8 cts. per lb. or ten if we find greece. We think no one would grumble at the price of 8 cents for carding merino wool, if they were acquainted with the great expense and difficulty attending it—in the first place the cost of the cards is more, as it requires much finer cards and they wear out a great deal sooner than for common wool, and also take much longer time to card the same number of pounds.
>
> The Sawing will also be reduced to suit the times—the following is a list of prices :
>
> For sawing ½ inch plank $0 50 per hundred.
> do   ⅝   55
> do   ¾   60
> do   ⅞   65
> do   1   70
> do   1¼   75
> do   1½   85
> do   1¾   90
> do   2   1 00
>
> All over two inches measuring side and edge at $1 per hundred—Laths and pailings measuring side and edge at the same price of plank the same thickness.
>
>   JOHN MEDARY.
> December 18.

1828 notice offering mill services at Robertson's
(later Muncaster's) Mill
(The Maryland and True American)

Rock Creek

Muncaster's Sawmill
(Library of Congress HABS)

In 1787, George Robertson advertised for his "runaway negro, Jeffery, who has been used to attend a mill."[17]

According to the last miller, William Dove, a "hermit" lived for a time in the foundation, which can still be seen by the side of the road at Meadowside Nature Center.

Across Muncaster Mill Road is the site of the dam, and farther upstream are traces of **Owen's Mill** which was described as an old sawmill in 1783. Located on the "Mt. Ararat" tract (a biblical reference to the resting place of Noah's ark), the race is located on the east bank above the creek. The mill was last noted on an 1838 map drawn by noted topographer John J. Abert.[18]

The uppermost mill on Rock Creek was **Bowie's Mill**, a small enterprise owned by Thomas J. Bowie. Part of "Flint Hill" farm, it was described in 1890 as "a grain and sawmill, in good repair with excellent water-power to which there is annexed a comfortable dwelling house for the miller."[19] After it was abandoned, William Dove, the last miller at Muncaster's Mill, used the foundation stones to build his home on Bowie Mill Road. The race and wheel pit are located west of the road on the south side of the branch on private property.

Bowie Mill
(Montgomery County Historical Society)

29

PATUXENT RIVER

As we enter Montgomery County from the southeast, the first mill site on this river was **Ridgely's Mill**, in the possession of Major Henry Ridgely in 1787.[1] Located on land patented to the Waters family in the mid-eighteenth century, the mill seems to have disappeared at an early date, although Ridgely descendants are shown in the area in maps of 1865 and 1878. The property is now part of the Rocky Gorge Reservoir north of Burtonsville.

At the old river crossing known as Snell's Bridge, was **Rawlings Mill**. Situated on the "Bear Garden" tract, the mill was established c.1800 by Quaker entrepreneur Richard Thomas, who also owned a mill at Brookeville. In 1820, the mill was in the hands of Gideon Davis and, by the 1870s, was advertised as the property of Benjamin Rawlings as a "merchant mill with fair water power and a large dwelling house...."[2]

Abandoned for years, the miller's log house was ultimately restored and now marks the location of the mill on private land at Tucker Lane east of Ashton.

Rawlings Mill House in 1974
(Photograph by the author)

Notice of sale of Rawlings Mill
(Montgomery County Sentinel, July 19, 1872)

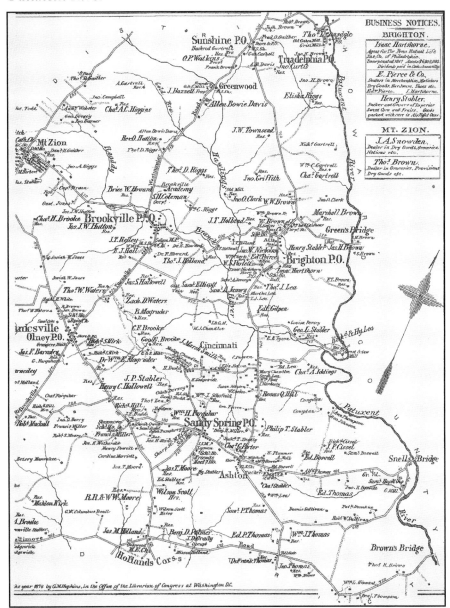

1879 Hopkins' Atlas, showing the southern portion of the Patuxent River Valley in Montgomery County[3]

Patuxent River

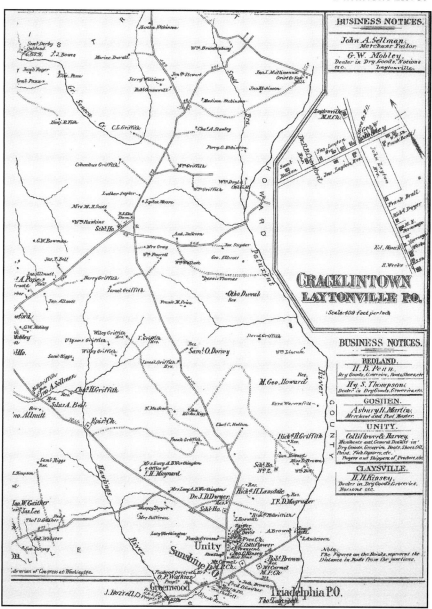

1879 Hopkins' Atlas, showing the northern portion of the Patuxent River Valley in Montgomery County[3]

Patuxent River

Upriver from **Rawlings Mill** is Haviland Mill Road, the site of **Leawood Mills**, operated first by Thomas Lea and later by Merrit Haviland. Featuring an unusual "tub wheel," it produced flour, meal and feed, among other products. A few stones and the miller's house are all that remain of this enterprise.[4]

Lea-Haviland Mill
(Sandy Spring Historical Society)

North of here, where Brighton Dam Road crosses the Patuxent River, was a tract patented in 1796 as "The Mill Seat," but no other mention of a mill at this location exists.

Little trace of an entire milling and manufacturing village remains at **Triadelphia**, named for three Quaker brothers-in-law. Their large stone cotton mills—along with grist, saw and cider mills, and a blacksmith shop—replaced Dr. Ephraim Howard's "tilting forge"[5] which had stood here since Revolutionary times. Founded in 1809, Triadelphia was a unique enterprise in the county that employed fifty-two women in the cotton mills alone. Last operated by the Lansdale family, it was finally inundated in the 1940s to create the Triadelphia Reservoir. Despite rumors of an Atlantis-like city beneath the waters, records show that the buildings were dismantled, and today only a cemetery remains as evidence of this lost town, located off Route 97 (Georgia Avenue) north of Sunshine.[6]

Triadelphia in the 1930s
(Library of Congress HABS)

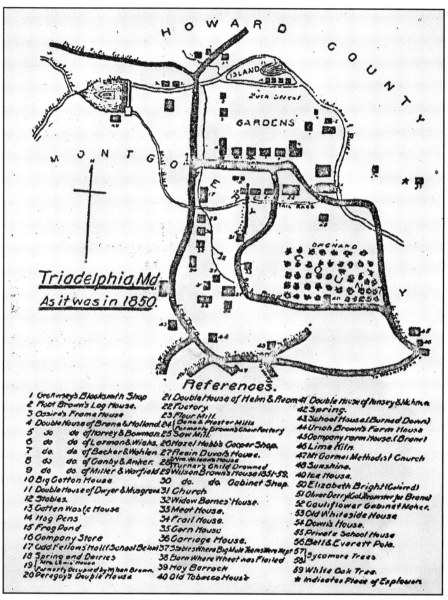

*From "Religious Telescope," published in Dayton, Ohio, on
August 23, 1911
(Reprinted from Maryland Historical Magazine)*

Patuxent River

On the west side of Georgia Avenue at the Howard County line was another Revolutionary period manufactory, **Gaither's Fulling Mill**, advertised by Henry Gaither in 1775 as on the Patuxent River and "now well-fixed . . . for fulling, shearing, pressing [wool], etc."[7] By the 1860s, the site was occupied by Alf Brown's Saw Mill. A remodeled stone house marks the location in Patuxent State Park today.

Henry Gaither owned three mills in 1783 including his "new" gristmill on the "Gaither's Forest" tract on Brown's Branch near Unity.[8] An overgrown race sits adjacent to Elton Farm Road at one of the most picturesque, but isolated, spots in the county.

Several miles upstream near Etchison is Hipsley Mill Road. Although the Hipsley Brothers did operate a mill in Brookeville at one time, this road leads to a mill that was actually just across the line in Howard County on the west side of the road. Near the abandoned junction of Halterman and Annapolis Rock Roads, however, stood Duvall's— later Doyle's—Mill.[9]

The next river crossing is Mullinix Mill Road, shown as the location of **Pigman's Mill** on a map of 1795 and later described as "Mershberger's Old Mill." Advertised as a grist and sawmill belonging to Ephraim Etchison in the 1830s, it was rebuilt in 1869 by the Mullinix family. According to the late Harold W. Mullinix, Sr., the mill burned in about 1920, but he recalled taking crops there

The miller's house at the site of the old Mullinix Mill in 1973
(Photograph by the author)

with his father and grandfather. There was also a cider mill and a family-owned store nearby.[10] An old wheel cog was uncovered when digging a pond, and the miller's house and mill site remain at the southeast corner of the road and river on public land.[11]

HAWLINGS RIVER

Although a tributary of the Patuxent River, the Hawlings River deserves a special place of its own because of its numerous milling enterprises. There is little doubt that the name is derived from the Holland family, who were early settlers along its banks, northeast of Brookeville. The date 1737 is said to mark the origin of **James Brooke's Mill**, located near the old Bladensburg Road, now New Hampshire Avenue. Along with his in-laws, the Snowden's, James Brooke was a large landowner and a savvy entrepreneur who had begun the mill with his brother-in-law, John Thomas. In 1756, he contracted to build a new mill and specified that he would pay millwright Thomas Leach in cash and iron from Snowden's Iron Works on the Patuxent River, near present-day Laurel. He also built a factory to make ship's biscuits and bread, and advertised in 1760 that he would deliver his products by wagon roads leading to the landings at Bladensburg, Georgetown and Elkridge.

Notice that James Brooke will carry on Ship's biscuit bakery trade (Maryland Gazette, June 1760)

In 1772, he announced his desire to sell his double-geared gristmill built almost twenty years earlier. Legend places the location of the mill on private land near the bridge on Gold Mine Road near Brookeville, and the site of the biscuit factory at the foot of Walnut Hill at Windswept Lane.[1]

James Brooke's notice to sell his gristmill on the Patuxent (Maryland Gazette, October 1772)

A later mill was established nearby at Delabrook, or Brothers Content, off Gold Mine Road. The **Chandlee Mill** property had descended to Mahlon Chandlee from his mother, Debra Brooke Chandlee, granddaughter of James Brooke. In 1783, James Brooke's mill had been described as "old"; after his death a year later, his children argued in court that the "water grist mill was in bad repair and the millstones nearly worn away." This new mill was originally a sawmill, but was later modified by master builder Chandlee to grind meal. The old stone miller's house can be seen across the road from the mill site at Chandlee Mill Road, where the Hawlings meets James Creek on parkland.[2]

Near the headwaters of James Creek northeast of Olney, near Montgomery General Hospital, is the site of **Brooke Grove Mill**, operated as a grist and sawmill by another remarkable Quaker family. The successful farm here eschewed slave labor, employing, among others, John Sinclair as a miller. The old frame mill disappeared from the scene by the early twentieth century, but the mill pond still remains as part of the new housing development.[3]

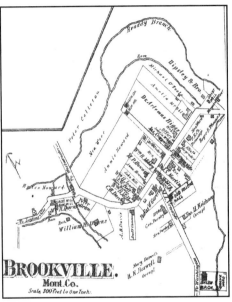

Hopkins' Atlas, 1879, showing Brookeville with mills at both ends of town

Moving north along present-day Georgia Avenue on the old road to Westminster, one encounters the town of Brookeville, site of two mills on Reddy Branch. When the British burned Washington in 1814, President Madison and his party took refuge in the home of postmaster Caleb Bentley and, while there, remarked at the peaceful appearance of the mills in the village.

Thomas' Mill, Brookeville
(Photograph courtesy of Sylvia Nash)

The first of these was **Thomas' Mill** located east of town and built in the 1790s. The second was **Newlin's Mill** on the west end of town. This mill was established in the 1800s and enjoined from grinding grains so as not to compete with Thomas' Mill. Instead, Newlin's Mill ground flax, castor and clover seed.[4]

Both mills operated for many years and were later operated by the Weer and Hipsley families, among others. On private land, the stone miller's house for Thomas' mill can be seen from the street on the east end of town, and the race from Newlin's Mill runs west along Brookeville Road towards Oakley Cabin.

Newlin's Mill, Brookeville
(Photograph courtesy of Sylvia Nash)

VALUABLE MILL PROPERTY FOR SALE OR RENT.—The subscriber offers for sale or for rent his Mill property, in Brookeville, Maryland, consisting of a stone mill-house, with one run of French burrs and one of country stones, east-iron gearing, in good order; miller's house and other outhouses, with about sixteen or seventeen acres of land, part of which is in cultivation.
This property is situated in one of the most desirable neighborhoods in the State of Maryland, being in the immediate vicinity of Sandy Spring, in Montgomery county, where the lands are in a high state of cultivation, large crops of wheat and other grain raised, and the quantity annually increasing, the inhabitants highly intelligent, moral, and many of them wealthy farmers. To a good Miller, with some capital, this is a most desirable situation, and will be sold or rented on fair terms. If not sold before *Monday, the 14th of June*, the property will then be for rent. To a responsible tenant the terms will be easy.
Communications addressed to the subscriber, in Alexandria, Va., will be attended to until *Saturday, June 6th*, after which he may be seen at the Mill until the 14th.
may 27—2aw2w   THOS. McCORMICK.

1820s for-rent notice for the Thomas/McCormick/Weer/Hipsley Mill
(Daily National Intelligencer)

As a result of the embargo placed on imported goods during the War of 1812, Quaker David Newlin also established the **Brookeville Woolen Factory** on the Hawlings River, northwest of present-day Brighton Dam Road. Among the products he advertised were "servants' clothes," a euphemism for apparel customarily provided to slaves by their owners. Not to be outdone, Richard

Thomas, also a Quaker, announced that he was fulling, dyeing and finishing cloth at his fulling mill in Brookeville in 1813.[5] The Newlin enterprise seems to have prevailed, however, as it was shown on maps for many years, albeit under different ownership. Elderly residents recalled bringing wool to the stone structure, that still stands adjacent to the miller's house on private property. Operated as a game preserve in the 1940s and a quarry in the 1950s, the mill was abandoned until being restored by several owners during the late 1970s and 1980s.

Greenwood Mill
(Photograph courtesy of Leonard Becraft)

North of Brookeville, where Georgia Avenue crosses the Hawlings River, is the site of **Greenwood Mills**, operated as part of Allen Bowie Davis' plantation that remains on the east side of the road here. The miller's house, that was covered in a stone veneer, also remains situated on a hill on the west side of the road. A plat of Greenwood plantation, surveyed in 1857, shows the mill, dam and race not only for this mill, but for the Brookeville Woolen Factory downstream as well.

The miller's house in Speck family photograph (left) and a 1930s photograph of Greenwood (right)
(Library of Congress HABS)

The plat also verifies the location of **Musgrove's Old Mill** mentioned in the 1783 tax assessment as being on the tract of "Treed Land."[6] According to the reminiscences of Lafayette Dwyer recorded in 1930, the mill was operated before and after the Civil War by Wilson Johnson, first as a slave and later as a free man.[7] In the winter of 1860, young Esther Davis was leaning over the wheel to get an icicle. When the mill started operation, the wheel caught her dress, which she immediately tore off, thus escaping certain death.

Last operated by the Speck family from western Maryland, the four-story frame structure was reportedly demolished during improvements to Georgia Avenue during the 1920s.[8]

Continuing upstream, just east of Hobbs Road near Unity are the ruins of **W. B. Gaither's Mill**, which was one of several mills owned by this family during the eighteenth and nineteenth centuries.[9]

> August 18.
>
> **WOOLLEN FACTORY**
> **FOR SALE.**
>
> BY virtue of a deed of trust from Jehu Price to the subscriber, will be exposed to Public sale
>
> *On Thursday the 30th of Aug. inst.*
> That extensive and excellent
> **WOOLLEN FACTORY,**
> and all the machinery thereunto belonging; together with 12¼ ACRES OF LAND, more or less; with a good Stone
> **DWELLING HOUSE,**
> a convenient barn, and other necessary buildings. This property is situated in a desirable neighborhood on Holland's River, in Montgomery county, one and a half miles north of Brookeville, and within a convenient distance of the Baltimore and Ohio Rail Road, and is well worthy the attention of manufacturers and men of capital.
>
> Sale to take place on the premises at 10 o'clock, A. M. at which time the terms will be made known.
>
> AMOS FARQUHAR, Trustee.

1832 announcement that the Brookeville Woollen Factory is to be sold
(Frederick-Town Herald)

An interesting nearby feature is a large dike of quartz rock similar to the better-known Annapolis Rock in nearby Howard County. The site of the mill is located on public parkland in the Rachel Carson Conservation Park.

PAINT BRANCH

One of the most unusual watersheds is the Paint Branch that flows southeast from Spencerville into Prince George's County. Despite its urbanization over the years, this creek remains remarkably picturesque and pristine, still capable of sustaining a trout population. Although few signs are visible, records reveal that it was once a thriving vale of small-scale rural industries. Below Route 29, near the old Naval Ordnance Lab with restricted access, stood **Harper's Woollen Factory** in the mid-nineteenth century. Irishman William Harper and his English wife, Lucretia, employed among others Robert Didenhover, whose family had operated a fulling mill on Muddy Branch years earlier. As Harper had been indebted to well-known millwright Leonard Weer of Brookeville, his property was eventually sold to a wealthy English woman, Alice Pilling, who years later conveyed a part of that land to Mary and George Harper "in consideration of respect that she had for the parents of George Harper and his family." Another mill at this location, possibly the same site as the later Harper's Woollen Factory, was listed in 1815 on the Yorkshire tract of

Lucretia Harper
(Photograph courtesy of James Sorensen)

Thomas Fawcett's 1831 announcement of wool production on Paint Branch
(Daily National Intelligencer)

43

Paint Branch

land, originally owned by Richard Lansdale, later by Daniel Porter, Edward Dawes and finally by Thomas Jenkins of Baltimore.[1]

Above this point on the south side of the old Columbia Pike is the site of **Lansdale's Mill**. Like William Harper, John W. Lansdale had borrowed money to finance his mills; when he defaulted, the 1833 advertisement described "a valuable mill property for sale," 21¼ acres of

> easy purchase and re-survey on 'James and Mary.' Two-story frame grist and merchant mill . . . valuable saw mill . . . part of the mill has been used for manufacturing purposes for some years past. Property sits on Paint Branch directly on the contemplated turnpike road from Ellicott's Mill to Washington City.[2]

Lansdale's Mill was built by Isaac Lancaster Lansdale and Benjamin Berry in the 1790s and is pictured in an 1830 roads document. It was also the

The etching "Old Mill on Paint Branch" by Charles Volkmar
(Worcester Art Museum)

subject of an etching by artist Charles Volkmar in 1859, after the mill had been abandoned. The "manufacturing purposes" mentioned in the advertisement were the work of Thomas Fawcett, who announced in 1831 that he was "still carding at J.W. Lansdale's mill on Paint Branch." The race can be seen near the ruins of the two old bridge structures on the north bank of the creek in Paint Branch Park.[3]

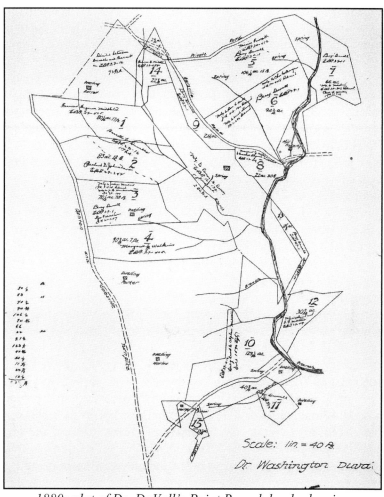

1880s plat of Dr. DuVall's Paint Branch lands showing mill property
(Montgomery County Historical Society)

Paint Branch

The mill was purchased at auction by William Holmes of "Montmorenci," a wealthy investor responsible for lending Lansdale the money to finance his mill. In an 1847 Maryland Chancery Court case, there is a mention of Holmes' "Mill Peace" tract on Paint Branch with "an old mill, a rotten dam, and good for nothing."[4] This property was sold to Dr. Washington Duvall of Fairview near Colesville, and almost 50 years later, was mentioned as on the new road (now Jackson Road) near White Oak "where there was formerly a mill dam." The aforesaid dam was the milldam north of Route 29, Old Columbia Pike, for Lansdale's Mill.

The Thomas Fawcett mentioned at Lansdale's Mill in 1831 was a native of Yorkshire, England, a region known for its wool manufacturing. He reportedly began his employment downstream at Bladensburg, where John W. Lansdale was also living in the early 1800s. The loss of Lansdale's mill due to foreclosure undoubtedly led to Fawcett's temporary move to the Oakland Woolen Mills, as it was called in Brookeville. In the meantime, Dr. Samuel Lukens had moved to Montgomery County from the Philadelphia area and had purchased land on Paint Branch, near present-day Fairland Road. In 1814, he advertised his property on Paint Branch, including "a geared saw-mill where either a fulling, cotton or woolen factory could be built onto the water wheel already built."[5]

Lukens' property remained unsold and after his death in 1824 was again advertised for sale. He had apparently followed his own advice as the property now included a "large merchant and grist mill. There was also lately a saw mill, which did the property a good business, in being one of the best lands for sawing in the county." It was further stated, "that water power is worth the attention of manufacturers." A picture of the mill appears in an 1830 plat accompanying the sale. The property was sold to Dr. Washington Duvall of Fairview, owner of another mill on the stream below at Old Annapolis Road, now Randolph Road. Duvall lent Thomas Fawcett the money to set up his equipment at Lukens' old mill and secured the machinery as collateral. By mid-century, Fawcett had purchased the mill, named it the **Paint Branch Woolen Factory** and was apparently making a decent living.[6]

After Fawcett's death in 1871, however, the entire house of cards collapsed, leaving his nine children plus seven of his deceased daughter's children to settle his indebted estate. In a bitter Equity Court case that dragged on for years, depositions were taken that revealed much about the mill. Son Benjamin testified that he had charge of the factory for more than twenty years, and that his brother Joseph had taken over, after 1868. He further noted that his father had begged him to take charge of the factory or he would be ruined, so Benjamin did and added, "I have sacrificed my life to it."[7]

Dr. Duvall had provided loans to keep the factory running, which in turn supported the family. Neighbors testified that the place was never farmed,

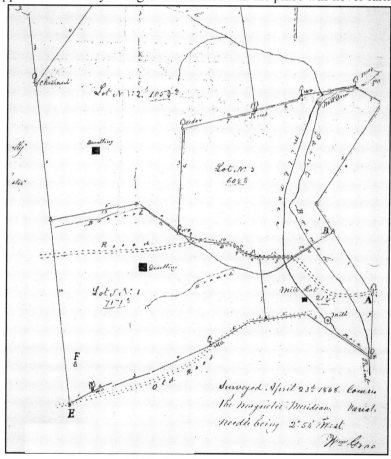

1868 plat of Fawcett's Mill
(Montgomery County Court House)

Paint Branch

with very little land cleared. Ben took a job as treasurer of the C & O Canal Company to keep his parents "from being thrown off the farm," but his sister Pinky replied, "Ben never thought them worthy of being consulted and that is where the trouble comes from. Women can sometimes understand as well as men." The property was sold for debts, and the survey showed that the mill site was just south of Fairland Road in Paint Branch Park. Ironically, the mills of Lukens, Fawcett and Dr. Duvall were all located on or adjacent to the **Snowden's Mill** tract, which had been surveyed for ironmonger Richard Snowden in 1723 and described as containing "a small mill thereon." This statement is the earliest reference to a mill in what is now Montgomery County.[8]

1773 advertisement for Valley Mill (Maryland Gazette)

While little else is known about Snowden's Mill, the history of its successors can be traced in a series of records. The mill that eventually became known as **Valley Mill** was located on present-day Randolph Road, formerly known as the old Annapolis Road, and was owned throughout the eighteenth century by a number of Scottish investors. In 1773, Ninian Edmonston advertised a "single geared grist mill with a bolting cloth." Twenty years later, German miller Peter Kemp arrived from Frederick to assemble his mill seat along the branch. As with nearby Lansdale's Mill, the intent

1783 advertisement for Valley Mill (Maryland Gazette)

was to take advantage of the proximity of the Old Columbia Road leading to the nation's new capital, and Kemp most likely incorporated Oliver Evans' new technology in his mill and built a small but elegant brick residence for himself.

This residence remains in Valley Mill Park, along with the race and foundation of the mill. Kemp trained his nephews in

Valley Mill, with the miller's house in the background, as they appeared in the 1930s (Library of Congress HABS)

the milling trade, and after his death they moved on to other mills, notably Kemp's Mill on Northwest Branch, west of Colesville. In 1835, they sold the Paint Branch mill to Dr. Washington Duvall, who acquired it as part of his Fairview plantation. It included the blacksmith's shop, operated by a mulatto slave named Isaac Bellows. Duvall had been born near Kensington, where his father owned the old Newport Mill. Duvall was a slave owner, and corn meal, provided from the mill, was an important source of food for slaves. Dr. Duvall died in 1874 after owning the mill property for almost 40 years.

Franklin Pilling purchased the property and rebuilt the mill, installing a Poole and Hunt turbine in place of the old-fashioned

Miller's house at Valley Mill during archaeological investigation of the mill, 1985 (Photograph by author)

water wheel. According to a later court deposition, he alleged that he had left a successful business in his native England at the urging of his aunt, Alice Pilling, who owned the large farm downstream on Paint Branch.

Frustrated at her failure to give him the deed to the farm, he was about to return home when his aunt prevailed upon him to stay, giving him the money to acquire and remodel Duvall's old mill. Franklin Pilling claimed that the money was a gift, but his aunt argued that it was a loan; and the court ruled in her favor, ordering the sale of the mill in 1886.

The poor location of the mill was a factor in its demise, as small country mills, overshadowed by large merchant mills in the grain belt of the Midwest, were starting to decline in this era. The mill was ultimately abandoned but stood as a ghostly ruins as late as 1940. By that time, it had become part of the Valley Mill Farm of Captain Winfield Scott Overton, a West Point classmate of General Conley, who lived at nearby Green Ridge Farm. The property descended to the Vierling and McEwan families, who operated a day camp there until the Maryland-National Capital Park and Planning Commission purchased the site for parkland in the 1970s.[9]

Only one mill is recorded as being on the Little Paint Branch, which was on nine acres of "Edmonston's Range," owned by Thomas Richardson in 1815 and Harriet Johnson in 1820. This tract is located east of Route 29 off Robey Road near the Prince George's County line.[10]

TRUSTEE'S SALE

OF

VALUABLE MILL PROPERTY.

BY VIRTUE of a Decree of the Circuit Court for Montgomery county, as a Court of Equity, passed in a cause in said Court wherein John W. Pilling is complainant and Franklin A. Pilling and Eliza A. Pilling, his wife, are defendants, the subscriber, as Trustee, will offer at public sale to the highest bidder, at the Court House door in the town of Rockville, in said county,

On TUESDAY, the 8th day of June, 1886,

at the hour of 12 o'clock, M., all the property decreed to be sold in said cause. This property is what was formerly known at Davall's Mill, and is located on Paint Branch where it crosses the public road leading from Colesville to Beltsville, on the Washington Branch of the Baltimore and Ohio Railroad, about two miles from Colesville, four from Beltsville, and thirteen miles from Washington, and contains

22¾ ACRES OF LAND,

more or less. This property is improved by two good

DWELLING HOUSES,

a Barn, Corn House, Carriage House and other outbuildings, and by a

SUBSTANTIAL FRAME MILL,

28x33 feet, three and a-half stories high, the lower story of which is stone. This Mill was built in 1879, and fitted up with new and improved machinery, including a Poole & Hunt latest improved turbine water wheel. It has three runs of stones, one for wheat, one for corn and one for chop, with all necessary machinery for making a high grade of flour, and has a capacity of two hundred bushels per day. The water power is ample and the property is in every respect desirable and is very valuable.

TERMS OF SALE, as prescribed by the Decree: The whole of the purchase money to be paid in cash on the day of sale or the ratification thereof by the Court; and upon the ratification of the sale by the Court and the payment of the whole purchase money, (and not before,) the Trustee will convey the property to the purchaser or purchasers thereof. Conveyancing at the cost of the purchaser.

JAMES B. HENDERSON,
May 14, 1886.   Trustee.

Printed at the "SENTINEL" office, Rockville, Md

Handbill announcing the sale of
Valley Mill in 1886
(Montgomery County Courthouse)

NORTHWEST BRANCH

This watershed flows south from the Sandy Spring to the Prince George's County line and eventually becomes the Eastern Branch of the Potomac River, commonly called the Anacostia River. When Walter Beall advertised his mills for sale in 1784, he claimed " it is well known to be one of the first seats on the Continent."[1] The mill site is known today as **Burnt Mills** on Columbia Pike or Route 29, and although it may indeed have burned at an early date, even "old timers" at the turn of the century could not recall a mill being burned.[2] That the location for a mill was a good one was indisputable, however, as the tract was patented as "Mill Seat" by Samuel Beall, Walter's father in 1745.

Charles Cheney's 1783 notice to sell his mill
(Maryland Journal, and Baltimore Advertiser)

Another mill, described as "old" in 1783, was owned by Charles Chaney on the "Hard Struggle" tract a mile and a half downstream, but had been acquired by Walter Beall by the following year.[3]

Due to its superior waterpower or "fall," the Burnt Mills seat was purchased in whole or in part by a number of investors, including the likes of Peter Kemp and Nathan Loughborough who had mills of their own

*Burnt Mills on Northwest Branch in 1914
(The Washington Star)*

elsewhere in the county.

The most enterprising of these owners, however, was James L. Bond, who acquired the mill in 1850 and developed it into the second largest flourmill in the county. By 1884, the mill was purchased by William Manakee who further improved the operation, converting it to a modern "roller mill." As a youth, Manakee had been taken into the home of Allen Bowie Davis of "Greenwood" near Brookeville and had learned the milling trade at the mill on that property and later in Washington, D. C. Eventually, he was sold half interest in the Burnt Mills by his father-in-law, James Bond.[4] Located in a rocky glen, the mill was the scene of a Fourth of July speech by famed orator William Jennings Bryan in the late 1800s. In addition, in

*Burnt Mills in the 1930s
(Photograph courtesy of the Historical Society of Washington, D.C.)*

Detailed description of Beall's Mill property in 1784 for-sale notice (Maryland Journal, and Baltimore Advertiser)

Public Sale, of a very valuable Estate.

To be SOLD, at PUBLIC VENDUE, on Monday the 27th day of September inst. (if not fair, the next fair day) at the dwelling-plantation of the subscriber, in Montgomery County, Maryland;

AN OVERSHOT GRIST-MILL, on the Northwest-Branch, with One Hundred Acres of Land laid off convenient thereto. It is well known to be one of the first seats on the Continent, the water having never been known to fail—a good and convenient dwelling-house—a large still-house, and a barn—an apple-orchard of about 200 good bearing trees. About 150 yards below, on the same stream and land, there is a Mill-seat, with more fall than the other, lying in Montgomery County Maryland, about 11 miles from George-Town, 7 from Bladensburg, and about 35 from Baltimore.——Also, my Dwelling-Plantation adjoining, with about Nine Hundred Acres of Land, now rented in three plantations.——If more suitable to the purchasers, Four Hundred Acres of Land will be conveniently laid off and sold with my Dwelling-Plantation. The other places will be sold as will best suit, together or separate. This Land adjoins the aforesaid Mill Tract.—— The improvements on my Dwelling-Plantation are as follow, viz. a good well-finished dwelling-house, with four good rooms below, and two rooms and a passage above, three good fire-places, a good cellar under the house, a convenient well-finished kitchen, with a large fire-place and bake-oven; a very large and good barn, corn-house, stables, Negro quarters, and other convenient houses; two good pailed yards to the dwelling-house; a large and good pailed garden; four very good apple-orchards, that will produce a large quantity of fruit; also, plenty of other fruit-trees, viz. peach, pear, cherry, damson, &c. Likewise, a Grist-Mill and Fifty Acres of Land, which I lately purchased of Charles Chaney, about a mile and a half below, on the same stream of the above-mentioned mill.——

One Hundred and Forty-six Acres of Land, whereon Thomas Wilmot lives, about four miles from George-Town.

Ninety-nine Acres and a Half of well-timbered Wood-Land, about a mile and a half from George-Town.

Nine Acres and a Quarter of Land, lying between and adjoining the water and George-Town, very convenient to said Town, and may be laid off into lots that will, undoubtedly, become very valuable.

Nineteen Acres and a Half of Land, lying adjoining on the West side of Rock-Creek, near its mouth, within a quarter of a mile of George-Town.

One Hundred Acres of well-timbered Wood-Land, which I lately purchased of Benedict Calvert, Esq; lying on the Northwest-Branch, about four miles from Bladensburg, in Prince-George's County.

Also, a Stock of Cattle, Hogs, and Sheep; and all sorts of plantation-utensils.

For the Mills and Lands, twelve months credit, on giving bond and approved security, if required, will be given for one third of the purchase-money; two years for one third more; and three years for the last payment. The interest on the whole to be paid annually.——If paid immediately, European Goods, or Negroes, will be taken for the whole, or any part thereof.——I will take part in military, continental, or state certificates; and for all sums of money paid down, Ten per cent. will be discounted.

The terms of sale for the Stock, and Plantation-Utensils, will be made known on the day of sale.

WALTER BEALL.

September 1, 1784.

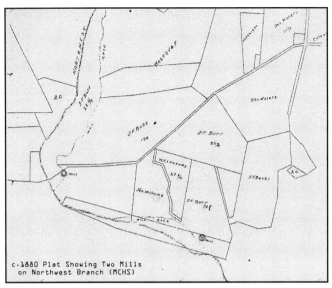

c. 1880 plat showing two mills on
Northwest Branch
(Montgomery County Historical Society)

1904, "Rough Rider" and president Teddy Roosevelt rode by horseback to the property and declared it "the most beautiful place around here (excepting Great Falls)."[5]

By 1928, the mills were abandoned and subsequently removed for the construction of the Robert Morse Water Filtration Plant, which provided safe drinking water for the growing suburban population. In recent years, the Washington Suburban Sanitary Commission conveyed the site to the Maryland-National Capital Park and Planning Commission for public parkland.[6]

Continuing upstream, one next encounters the site of **Kemp's Mill** at Randolph Road, formerly the Old Annapolis Road. A plat from about 1880 actually shows two mills near this location, and nineteenth century tax records list additional sawmills and a tan yard nearby.[7]

The primary mill at this location, however, dates to before 1800 and was established by prominent Quaker, Evan Thomas, who lived at "Mt. Radnor" near Colesville. Thomas leased the mill to Thomas Brown, but by 1820, Aaron Dyer was the owner. The small cluster of industries here evolved into a community known as Claysville. Only the Kemp name remains, even though their relatives, the Valdenars, Leckliders and Zeiglers, were among the later owners or operators.

Misfortune struck at the mill more than once: a customer was killed by a tree falling near the sawmill in 1873, a storm "worse than the Johnstown Flood" greatly damaged the mill in 1902, and in 1919 the mill was destroyed by fire thought to be arson. Although road construction has heavily impacted the millrace in recent years, traces of it can be found in the Kemp Mill Park to this day.[8]

1930s photograph of the old site of Kemp's Mill (Photograph courtesy of the Historical Society of Washington, D.C.)

Farther up the branch, in the stream valley park adjacent to "Woodlawn," was the location of **Birdsall's Mill**, reportedly operated by two Quaker brothers in the early 1800s. An 1831 deed mentions that Andrew Birdsall was "now of the County of Loudoun, and the State of Virginia."[9] Long abandoned, its location in the headwaters of the branch made local farmers joke that they would have to carry water in their caps to make it run. When the brick walkway at "Woodlawn" was constructed in the 1980s, the millstones were discovered, apparently having been used as a mounting block for riders on horseback.

CABIN JOHN CREEK

Flowing south from Rockville to the Potomac River community of Cabin John, this watershed contained a surprising collection of early mills, of which few traces remain. Despite various legends to the contrary, records indicate that the name of the stream is derived from the original "Captain John's Run." Near the intersection of Booth's Branch (also mispronounced as "Booze Branch") was **Magruder's Mill** on the "Mills Use" tract that belonged to Samuel Magruder III and was described in 1783 as "old." When advertised for sale in 1791, the property was noted being "where formerly stood a mill."[1]

Upstream from this location at the old River Road and the (later) Seven Locks Road, which leads to the C & O Canal, stood other mills owned by the Magruders, who settled the area in the early 1700s. The first recorded mill near this location was actually built for **Zachariah White**, who advertised his mill on Captain John's Run in 1769, describing it as "about 10 miles from George Town, 30 x 40 feet with a stone house and a stone dam."[2] Zachariah and James White were among the first to speculate on mills in the county, owning several others on Rock Creek and the Little Monocacy.

Notice of White's Mill on Captain John's Run for sale in 1769
(Maryland Gazette)

The Whites had purchased land here from Dr. James Doull, who had been assembling property "near the bridge on Captain John's Run" since the 1740s. By 1784, he had conveyed to his stepson, James Offutt, 20 acres "where said Offutt's watermill stands."[3] The mill seat had been resurveyed as " Doull's Park." It had apparently declined in value by the time James' son sold his interest in it, having moved to Kentucky like so many young men of that era.[4]

During the same time period in which Offutt was operating a grist and sawmill, Major Samuel Wade Magruder owned a fulling mill upstream on seven and a half acres of "Hobson's Choice," another of Dr. Doull's tracts that he had sold to the Whites. "Hobson's Choice" was a popular expression at the time, that essentially meant no choice at all. The Magruders were of Scottish origins and active patriots in the Revolution. The Major had made his home at "Locust Grove" and announced in a 1791 Georgetown paper that

> FOR SALE,
> THE one half of that valuable mi property, known by the name of
> Cabbin John Mills,
> Situated on a large Creek by th[e] name, and immediately on the mai[n] road leading from Georgetow[n] the Mouth of Monocacy, and wit[hin] two miles of the Potomac, b[y] means of which any quantity of grai[n] may at all times be had. Ther[e] are thirty three acres of land attac[h]ed to the mill seat chiefly in woo[d] The Mill house is 40 by 60 fee[t] three stories high, and built of th[e] very best materials. There a[re] two pair of first rate burrs in th[e] Mill, calculated to manufacture f[r]o[m] 40 to 70 barrels of flour each day.— The works are generally in good re[pair], there are also a good Miller house, and some other small building[s] on the Mill Seat. This is considere[d] among the most valuable Mill pr[o]perties in the State of Maryland.— Only a small portion of the purcha[se] money will be required in hand, f[or] the balance of which a credit of 4, or 6 years will be given; the purcha[s]er to give bond, properly secured; an[d] pay the interest annually.

August 7, 1822 notice of sale of Cabbin John Mills (Rockville True American) he had his fulling mill "in complete order and . . . will dress and dye cloth in any manner directed." [5]

While Magruder's children inherited his estate the following year, they do not seem to have acquired his business acumen. Son Patrick had attended Princeton and became a newspaperman. Despite stinging criticism from the rival *Frederick-Town Herald,* he was elected to both state and national political offices. He was appointed both Clerk of the United States House of Representatives and Librarian of Congress by Thomas Jefferson in 1807. [6] Soon after, he proceeded to build "that elegant stone mill house called **Cabin John Mills**, a 40 x 60 [foot] structure . . . immediately on the main road leading from Georgetown to the Mouth of Monocacy . . . ."[7]

A series of misfortunes soon overcame Patrick Magruder, however, causing his expensive mill to be known to his detractors as "Magruder's Folly." Several bitter lawsuits reveal the rivalry among his brothers. According to court testimony, George Magruder had approached a third brother, Warren, in 1813 alleging that he wanted to buy the old fulling mill seat that Warren had inherited from their father. George alleged that he intended to build a small mill for his own use, and that their brother Patrick had "ruined" him and that he (George) would cut off communication with Warren if the latter would not sell him the property.

Warren reluctantly sold the tract to George but later brought suit charging that George had deceived him and was actually acting as an agent for their brother Patrick, who was desperate to sell unencumbered shares of his Cabin John Mills and needed the old fulling mill site, as it would be flooded by his milldam.

A subsequent lawsuit by Warren Magruder and Michael Letton alleged that slaves hired by Patrick to work on his milldam had drowned in a leaky boat, and they were demanding payment for their property. Depositions taken at the mill reveal the harsh conditions that prevailed in the county at that time, including incidents of drunkenness, cockfights and slave whippings. Acting as an agent for his father, Brice Letton accused a neighbor of whipping a slave at Rabbitt's Cross Roads (now Wildwood on Old Georgetown Road). Ironically, Brice Letton was later identified as the model for Simon Legree, the cruel overseer in Harriet Beecher Stowe's book, *Uncle Tom's Cabin*.[8]

Cabin John Creek

The crowning blow came in 1815 when Patrick Magruder was forced to resign his position as Librarian of Congress as a result of questionable use of library funds and the loss of important documents when the British burned the Capitol, which housed the library during the War of 1812. Saddled with judgments, he was insolvent until his death four years later.[9] He was buried at his wife's ancestral home, "Sweden," near Petersburg, Virginia.[10]

The mill was seized by the sheriff to settle Magruder's debts and passed through several owners—including Andrew Way, who owned a glass manufactory in Washington. It operated as a paper mill before burning in 1857. The remaining stone foundation was used for a barn that stood at the adjacent quarries for years. Within recent memory, the miller's house sat on a hill west of the creek, on private land.[11]

Late nineteenth century photograph of Bell's Mills
(Montgomery County Historical Society)

East of the creek, at River and Seven Locks roads, stands an old, privately owned house known as "Stoneyhurst" (for the Stone family that owned the quarries of the same name). The house was built in the 1700s by Samuel Brewer Magruder, who owned yet another mill on Cabin John Creek nearby. In an 1816 sheriff's sale, mention was made of "**Samuel B.**

Magruder's Mill," and in his will, probated two years later, Samuel left his "new Mills" to his son Walter, who was listed as owning a mill on 302 acres of "Salem," a resurvey tract that lies primarily south of River Road.[12]

To the north along Seven Locks Road, where it intersects with present-day Democracy Boulevard, is the site of **Bell's Mill**, originally built by Lloyd Magruder, on part of Samuel Wade Magruder's "Locust Grove" plantation. It became the property of son Lloyd Magruder, who had also acquired the notorious seven and a half acres of "Hobson's Choice" downstream, which had been his brothers' undoing. Like his brothers, Lloyd was deeply in debt and the mill, described as being "on a fine stream of water" was eventually sold out of the family after his death in 1836.[13] It was later known as Orndorff's, and still later, Bell's Mill, for which the present Bell's Mill Road is named.

By 1936, only the foundation stones remained, and construction of the intersection has since obliterated the site.[14]

Also largely destroyed by highway construction in recent years was the site of **O'Neal's Mill**, in Cabin John Stream Valley Park at the southeast corner of Interstate I-270 and Montrose Road.[15]

Photograph of Locust Grove Mansion, 1975
(Photograph by author)

Cabin John Creek

On a branch of the creek at Tilden Lane is the site of **Boone's Mill**. The race is still visible high on the bank opposite Tilden Woods Recreation Center. Assessed for a tanning house in 1783, Isaiah Boone in 1800 declared that he was selling his plantation on Cabin John Creek "one mile from the old George Town/Frederick Road and three from Montgomery Court House." The property at the time contained two stone dwelling houses, two gristmills and one sawmill, with the admonition that "no mills can be built higher up the branch . . . ."[16] An old millstone could still be seen at the nearby "Holly Oaks" estate in the 1970s.

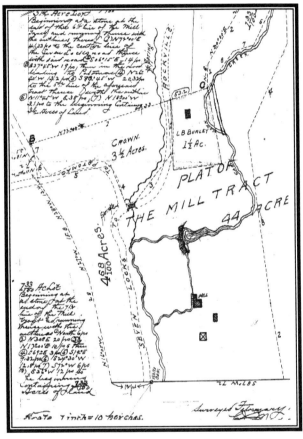

Early twentieth century plat of Bell's Mills
(Montgomery County Historical Society)

 # WATTS BRANCH

When Walter Evans patented a tract of land near the mouth of Watts Branch in 1752, reference was made to an "olde saw mill" which may explain the name "Saw Mill Creek" on early eighteenth century maps.[1] Although no mill was listed at this location in the tax assessment of 1783, George Washington mentions stopping at Mr. **Brooke Beall's Mill** in 1785, and the following year Brooke Beall willed his mill to his son Upton.[2] In 1830, Rockville tavern keeper Adam Robb was advertising for rent "the mill and dwelling belonging to the late Upton Beall at the Mouth of Watts Branch, the dwelling now occupied as a tavern."[3] By 1879, the property was shown on a map as "Beall's Old Mill," and long time resident Otis Swain recalled a roofless structure as late as 1910.[4] Situated on a tract of land called "Beallmount" opposite Beall Mountain Road at River Road, the race is still visible on public land.

Upstream, at the intersection of Glen and Glen Mill roads on public land, is the site of **Glen Mill,** located on the "Claggett's Folly" and "Brother's Industry" tracts. In 1820, David Claggett was assessed for a "new mill" here. Richard Gatton and Thomas Offutt also owned mills nearby.[5] In 1828, John Myers advertised that he had rented the late Offutt's Mill and would conduct a "country crest (*sic*)

Glen Mill
(Photograph by A. B. Veirs)

and saw mill" in conjunction with wagon and coach making.[6] By 1833, Claggett's Glen Mill had become the property of Rockville businessman John Braddock, and Charles Beckwith announced that he was "still carding wool at his old stand" there.[7] In an 1850 auction to satisfy the debts of Braddock, the Glen Mill was referred to as "Beckwith's grist and saw mill . . . in good repair and in the hands of an active manager would do a large and profitable business."[8] The mill was purchased for $700 by William Gamble. A decade later, a Mr. Creamer was calling for wool to be carded at Mr. Gamble's Mill, just as Charles Beckwith had done twenty years earlier. It is interesting to note that the young John Myers and his brother were still living nearby and listed in the census as "miller" and "wheelwright."[9]

Glen Mill was subsequently purchased by Zachariah Pumphrey, who was nearly fifty years of age when he came to the neighborhood from Germantown. He became Postmaster at Glen in 1892 and married Miss Lucy Peters, whose family updated the mill with modern rollers in 1890, according to the *Montgomery County Sentinel*, December 19, 1890.

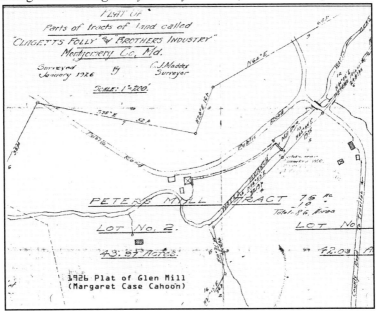

1926 plat of Glen Mill
(Courtesy of Margaret Chase Cahoon)

The Case family was the last owners of Glen Mill, which stood until the 1950s, when it was destroyed by fire.[10]

Upstream, near the county seat at Rockville, was **Wooton's Mill**. In 1842, Turner Wooton advertised for a "wright" to build a mill. By 1850, miller Benjamin Sparrow was renting it from the Wootons; he ground meal on one run of stones, and sawed lumber. A later miller was Salathiel Mullican. In 1905, the property became the country retreat of Smithsonian artist-topographer and curator William Henry Holmes.[11] The mill reportedly ceased operation at about the time it was purchased by the Veirs family in 1919. Today, the site is encompassed in Wooton's Mill Park, off Watts Branch Parkway. The park is owned by the city of Rockville.

One more mill apparently existed at the headwaters of this branch. A newspaper of 1788 mentions a mill belonging to James Perry, described in 1811 as being "two miles from the Court House on the main road to the Mouth of the Monocacy." It included a large brick dwelling house. An 1828 boundary document mentions "**Perry's Old Mill** on the Rockville-Darnestown Road." An 1882 account

Wooton's Mill on Watts Branch
(Photograph courtesy of the Historical Society of Washington, D.C.)

recalled that the nearest mill to Rockville was on Watts Creek; it was owned by Mr. Perry and was on the property owned by Mr. Stonestreet.[12] These descriptions would place it as part of the Thomas Farm, which is now undergoing private development along Route 28.

A FARM AND MILLS, FOR SALE.

AGREEABLY to the last Will and Testament of *Henry Strause*, late of Montgomery county, deceased, the subscriber will offer, at public sale, on the premises—

On Thursday 4th March, if fair, if not, the next fair day,

The Farm & Mills,

situated within 2 miles of Rockville, and about 2 miles from the contemplated route of the Potomac Canal, on the road leading to the mouth of Monocacy, containing

430 Acres, more or less,

with a sufficiency of Wood Land. The improvements are, a good Brick Dwelling HOUSE, one story, with a Kitchen and Spring House, and other out buildings; a Barn, a Blacksmith Shop, and Still house; two apple orchards and two peach orchards, of excellent fruit; a

Grist Mill and Saw Mill,

and a miller's house convenient to the mill. The above farm is well watered. The mill property will admit of being divided from the farm. The terms will be, one third of the purchase money on the first day of April next, when possession will be given—and the balance in two equal annual payments, with interest from the day of sale; & on payment of the last instalment a good title will be made. It is deemed unnecessary to give a further description, as it is presumed that any person wishing to purchase, will first view the property. Mr. Price, who resides on the farm, will show the property. The sale will commence at 2 o'clock P. M.

MATTHEW MURRAY,
Acting Executor.
January 13.   11—ts.

N. B. The above property is subject to the Dower of Mrs. C. Strause therein, but the same can be had by the purchaser, on terms which will be made known at the time of sale. If the above property is not sold on said day, it will then be offered for Rent.

1824 announcement that Perry's Old Mill is for sale (The Herald and Torch Light, Hagerstown, MD)

MUDDY BRANCH

Just below River Road on the west bank of the Muddy Branch are the faint traces of an early mill that had previously gone unnoticed due to its absence from maps. An advertisement in the *Maryland Gazette* in 1782 reveals, however, the existence of a "243 acre plantation with an overshot grist mill and a saw mill . . . some-thing out of repair at the present . . . ." The tract was described as being at the "mouth of a Branch called the Muddy Branch . . . ." It was being sold by C. **Wheeler** of Loudoun County, Virginia, whose home plantation was on "Patowmack River opposite to the mouth of Monocacy creek . . . ."[1]

September 19, 1783, notice of a gristmill on Muddy Branch to be sold

The next mention of this mill is in a lease executed in 1813 from the Reverend Mr. John Brackenridge of Washington, D. C., to William Dydenhover. Two years later, Mr. Dydenhover was advertising services available at his fulling mill at the mouth of Muddy Branch.[2] Dydenhover had come from Frederick, where he was reported to be operating a fulling mill in 1808. It was not surprising then that he was still picking up cloth at Frederick, Buckeystown and "The Manor"—all in Frederick County.[3] The last mention of the mill was in 1901, when a real estate advertisement mentioned "an old mill site" on the property.[4] This site is on county parkland.

Moving upstream, to where Muddy Branch intersects with **Query Mill** Road, you can find the eighteenth century grist and sawmill of Nicholas Query, who had immigrated to Maryland from Germany. He had acquired the mill seat from Samuel Boone, who had operated a sawmill during the

69

Muddy Branch

1700s. Query died at the age of 74 and is buried in a nearby family graveyard. In 1795, his sons were selling their "excellent" mill seat with a gristmill "in good repair," located about eight miles from Montgomery Court House.[5] In 1796, mention is made of Ray's "former gristmill," but by 1820, all of these mills had disappeared from public records.[6] The site of the mill cannot be found today.

A drawing of Beall & Lackland's Union Mills appears in an 1802 road petition, and by 1818 his heirs were selling the property, including a large brick dwelling house on Muddy Branch, six or seven miles from Montgomery Court House. A decade later, it was further described as containing "a large frame mill house, sawmill, cooper's shop, miller's house etc" on 19 acres of land.[7]

This property later became known as Glenwood Mills, under the ownership of John L. **Dufief**, who also owned a warehouse on the C & O Canal to store grain. Although a Dufief Mill Road

1818 notice of Lackland's Mills for sale
(Daily National Intelligencer, 1818)

exists nearby, the mill actually sat on Turkey Foot Road, the unusual name reflecting the shape of the original winding trail to Darnestown.[8]
These mills were described in 1866 as being built of the best materials, including a slate roof (which was reportedly placed later on Darby's Mill at Seneca). During the Civil War, both armies visited the mill seeking information and supplies.[9] The site of the dam and race can still be found today on public land on Muddy Branch at Turkey Foot Road. The old brick mansion house was located on nearby Belvedere Farm, scene of the Potomac Steeplechase races for years. It was torn down to make way for the current structure in 1941.[10]

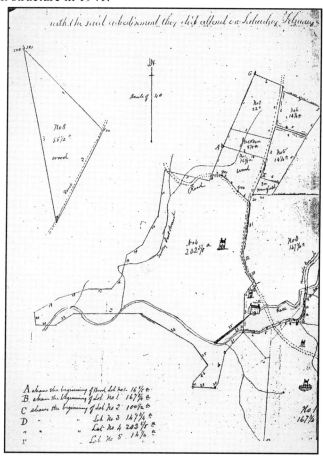

1878 plat of DuFief's Glenwood Mills
(Montgomery County Courthouse)

Muddy Branch

*1975 photograph of former site of DuFief's Mill on Turkey Foot Road
(Photograph by the author)*

BENNETT AND LITTLE BENNETT CREEKS

The Bennett and Little Bennett watersheds flow northwest into the Monocacy River Basin. The only known mill to have operated in Montgomery County on Bennett's Creek was the **Mill at Browningsville,** west of Damascus at the Frederick County line. Reportedly begun in 1818 by the Reverend "Jimmy" Day, who founded the nearby Methodist Church, the mill is on the tax records for that year with Thomas Duvall and George Kemp as owners "of a mill on 24 acres near the lands of James Day."[1] By the 1830s, it was being offered for sale by Eli Brashear, described as "a grist and saw mill, the machinery perfect, and adjoining the lands of Rev. James Day on 24 acres."[2]

By the late nineteenth century, the Browningsville mill was in the hands of William Turner until it burned in 1901.[3] Operations were resumed in 1908 by the Gladhill family. The Gladhills, who are well-known for their farming and civic endeavors, provided the accompanying photo of the family making apple butter at the mill in 1949. The mill had ceased to operate by then, with the machinery being used for scrap in the war effort. The mill building reportedly stood as late as the 1950s, but today only the part-log miller's house remains (on private property). The race is barely visible along Clarksburg Road, having been grazed over by cattle.[4]

1832 advertisement announcing the sale of the Reverend Jimmy Day's mill property in Browningsville (Frederick-Town Herald)

73

The earliest and most significant mill to operate on Little Bennett Creek was **Hyattstown Mill**, which was in existence at the time of the founding of Hyattstown in 1798. Located adjacent to the "Great Road," it was connected to a series of interdependent rural industries that shared the water power of Little Bennett and included a tan yard, bone mill and distillery.[5]

Hyattstown Mill on Little Bennett (Montgomery County Historical Society)

The Hyattstown Mills were variously owned by the Darby, Tabler and Dutrow families, and were remodeled or rebuilt over the years—the last time being after a disastrous fire in 1918, according to the miller.[6] Along with the adjoining miller's house, the mill, which ceased operation in 1937, was restored as part of the 3,600 acre Little Bennett Regional Park in 1990. It is currently used as a non-profit arts center; a sculpture trail has been developed along the old millrace that parallels Hyattstown Mill Road.[7]

Also in Little Bennett Park, at the intersection of Hyattstown Mill and Prescott Roads, are the ruins of **Zeigler's Bone and Sawmill.** The valley here was not well suited to farming, so other resources were exploited, including animal bones for fertilizer and tree bark and sumac leaves for use in the tan yard downstream at Hyattstown.

Gladhill family making apple butter at the mill in 1949 (Photograph courtesy of Bernardine Gladhill Beall)

A stone foundation marks the wheel-pit and water-filled tailrace, while the headrace extends for some distance along the road after crossing the pedestrian bridge.

The next mill along Little Bennett Creek was **Wilson's Sawmill** dating from the late 1800s. The race can be seen in the park, southwest of the Clarksburg Road crossing.

Farther upstream at Burnt Hill Road is the site of King's Distillery, which produced whiskey in the late 1800s. Maryland was known for its rye whiskey during this period, and the product was kept here in a warehouse before being shipped in barrels to Baltimore. The King family also advertised that corn whiskey was available for the help at harvest time.[8] The brick warehouse remained on site until purchased for parkland in the 1960s.

King's Mill in King's Vallley
(Photograph courtesy of Marguerite Appleby)

Bennett and Little Bennett Creeks

Across the road from the distillery is the race for **King's Grist and Sawmill** along Kingstead Road. The mill was located at the Clayton family property, where the Luther G. King house remains on private land. This area is historically known as King's Valley after John Duckett King who settled here in the late 1700s.[9] His old homestead is at Kingstead Farms, famous for its Holstein dairy cows. Above this point, the waters of Little Bennett are insufficient to power any more mills.

LITTLE MONOCACY RIVER

Although their geographic location makes them less well known than other more populated areas, the valleys of the Little Monocacy River were located in the heart of a thriving grain-growing region for over two centuries. There was a series of mills that processed grain and other products along these banks, although scant evidence of their existence remains today.

Zachariah White, who bought and sold mills on Rock Creek and Cabin John Creek in the eighteenth century, also advertised his "new mill" on the Little Monocacy, which he sold to Georgetown investors William and Francis Deakins in 1772.[1] The latter was assessed for "a good grist mill with a large stone mill house and grainery." In 1783, the land was resurveyed as "Mount Carmel." In 1790, Francis Deakins observed that "Our farmers will depend on Indian corn to support their families because the very high price of wheat will send every bushel out of the county."[2] Writing to Deakins in 1794 in regard to his adjacent "Woodstock" property, George Washington instructed that he "should greatly prefer the cultivation of wheat to tobacco, on those lands . . . ."[3]

Apparently James White became the owner of the mill, along with 300 acres and a dwelling house, described as being contiguous to the Monocacy and Georgetown Road.[4] (It is interesting to note that a Nathan White also owned a mill on the nearby "Hope Well" tract.) **Richard Gott** ultimately acquired the Mt. Carmel Mill Seat, and an early photograph of the mill shows a large stone structure, which was reportedly razed by 1915 to make way for State Route 28.[5] Other stone ruins and the race can be seen adjacent along the north side of the road to this day. Mount Carmel, the old Gott homestead located across the street, was the scene of a number of Civil War incidents, as the Gott's four sons-in-law (including Elijah Veirs White himself) were members of White's Confederate "Comanches."[6]

Near Beallsville along Route 28, was **Webster's Mill,** located on private property on the Spring Branch. This was a small mill associated with the "Eleven Brothers" tract owned by the White and Jones families. The millrace clings to a wooded hillside on the west side of Route 28; the sandstone miller's house—although greatly altered—sits directly on the road to the east side, marking the location of the mill. Gott's Mill was

Little Monocacy River

located beyond this location, after the bend in the road towards Dickerson. Leading from the center of Dickerson is Big Woods Road, which descends to the main branch of the Little Monocacy. It was at this junction that **Daniel Price** constructed a woolen factory with his son in the mid-nineteenth century. Earlier he had operated a grist and sawmill, but by 1850 he was carding, fulling and dyeing cloth.[7] In addition, he advertised a decade later that wool would continue to be picked up at Poolesville and Clarksburg. The millrace remains, along with the low-rise concrete dam on the north side of the stream, on private property.

Upstream, where the old Mouth of Monocacy Road crosses under the stone arches of the Little Monocacy railroad viaduct, was the site of the enduring **Oakland Mills**. This road was once a significant transportation link between Upper Montgomery County and nearby Frederick and Loudoun counties to the grain port of Baltimore. Both the road and the mill faded with the decline of wheat growing and the arrival of the railroad here in the 1870s.

One hundred years earlier, however, according to the tax record of 1783, Thomas Morton owned "a good grist mill on a fine stream of water" at this location.[8] The Oakland Mills, as they came to be known, were actively traded over the years. In 1817, they were described by Eli Dorsey, Jr., as a "newly built brick merchant mill 46 feet square with two pairs of

> Mills for Sale.
>
> I AM still desirous of selling my Mills with 100 acres of Land, in Montgomery county, lying upon the new-cut road, leading from the Mouth of Monocofy to Baltimore; as also my part of the Mills held in common with Mr. Thomas Morton, on the said road and near the Mouth of Monocofy. Mr. Morton's part of the Mills may also be had if wanted by the purchaser of my part. I also wish to sell 50 acres of Land in Frederick county, adjoining to Mr. Ralph Brook's land, on which there is a Settlement. The terms of sale will be easy, having lately made a purchase of other lands, I will now give a good bargain to a purchaser.—For further particulars, enquire of those living on the different places, or of
>
>   G. DAVIS.
>
> August 4, 1802.

1802 advertisement for sale of Morton's Mills on the "New Wheat Road" at the mouth of the Monocacy (Frederick-Town Herald)

five foot-burrs, one pair of 4½-foot country stones, etc."[9] The property also featured a plaster mill, which produced a popular fertilizer during that era. Located on the tract known as "Bealls Good Will," the mill seat was known for its large dam that was described as being upwards of 20 acres. This mill was featured in maps of the 1870s, when it was known as Major Hempstone's "Old Brick Mill."[10]

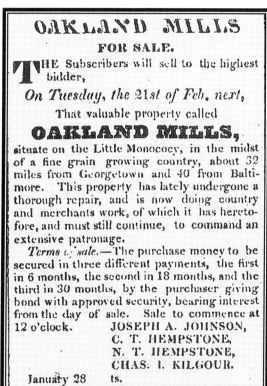

1832 advertisement for the same property then known as Oakland Mills
(Frederick-Town Herald)

The large mill pond also appears in a late eighteenth century plat of the real estate of Joseph Harris, near present-day Barnesville. Originally known as "White Oak Swamp," the land was re-surveyed by Harris in the late 1700s to form a 1200-acre tract (later referred to as 120 acres) known as "Mt. Zion." Although the plat erroneously labels the stream "Seneca," other land records confirm that it was actually the Little Monocacy River. The mill belonged to Thomas Morton, listed earlier.[11] The site is located on private land.

Another mill, located farther upstream, was shown on the same plat. When Joseph Harris died in 1797, his will bequeathed a grist and sawmill to his son, Jesse. According to tax assessments in 1820, **Robert Lyles** eventually became the owner of the "old mill on 120 acres of Mt. Zion."

Little Monocacy River

An extensive Equity Court case describes a bitter dispute between neighbors after Lyles defaulted on his payments to John Sprigg in 1822. The property was ordered sold by the sheriff. It was reported that Lyles' wife was forced to sell personal property, including her family Bible. The morning of the sale, Mr. Sprigg sent a bottle of whiskey to Mr. Lyles. Sprigg had gone to see Robert's father, Dr. Richard Lyles, before the sale,

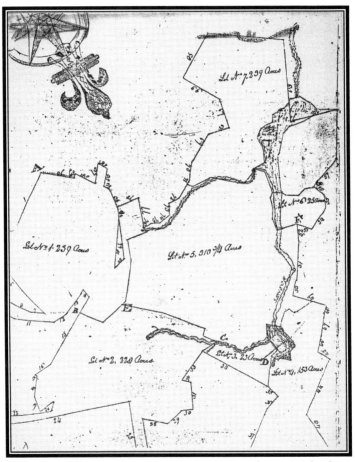

1797 plat of the lands of Joseph Harris, showing the large mill pond and the smaller pond for Lyles' Mill, on a stream incorrectly labeled "Seneca"
(Montgomery County Courthouse)

urging him to buy the mill property because, if he did not "Leonard Hayes (*sic*), would and would turn Robert's family out of house and home."[12]

Dr. Lyles eventually purchased the farm, although court testimony noted that by this time Little Monocacy was but "a weak stream of water… [which] fails in some manner in dry season." Nevertheless, Robert Lyles seems to have prevailed, as he advertised one hundred and twenty acres of Mt. Zion with a mill or mill seat "at the foot of Sugarloaf Mountain" for sale in 1844, although by this time the mill had apparently ceased operation.[13] An 1876 mention of Patrick McDade's "old mill" corresponds to this location on Harris Road and probably reflects McDade's status as a renter rather than an owner.[14] The mill site is on private land.

The last (and perhaps least known) mill on the Little Monocacy was **Ward's Mill**, probably the same as described as "W. Williams Mill, two and one-half miles west of Hyattstown," where local residents were reported to be ice-skating on the mill pond in 1890.[15] The site, today on private property, is marked by the race at the south side of Old Hundred Road.

> **FARM**
> **AT PRIVATE SALE.**
> I WILL sell, at Private Sale, a valuable FARM in Montgomery county, Maryland. It lies on the Little Monocacy, about 1¼ miles from Barnesville, on the road leading to Greenfield Mills, and about 3 miles from the Chesapeake and Ohio Canal, and contains
> **120 ACRES OF LAND;**
> 25 in Wood and 20 in Meadow. The soil is of good quality and the farm well watered—with a comfortable DWELLING HOUSE, STABLE, &c. and a never-failing Spring of Water convenient to the dwelling.
> There is a good MILL SEAT on the farm with the dam built and race dug, and from the great quantity of timber in its vicinity—being at the foot of the Sugar Loaf mountain—would be an excellent site for a saw-mill; also, for a distillery, factory, grist-mill, &c.
> The terms, which will be liberal, will be made known on application to the subscriber, residing in Poolsville.
> ROBERT LYLES.
> January 17, 1844—tf

1844 advertisement for the sale of Lyles' Mill
(Montgomery County Journal)

81

LITTLE FALLS BRANCH

The Little Falls Branch flows southwest from Bethesda into the Potomac River near the District line. The falls were the last barrier to river commerce before reaching the port of Georgetown, and considerable efforts were made to circumnavigate them, first by the old Potomac Canal and later by the C & O Canal. The area around the mouth of Little Falls Branch was a natural location for a number of mills, distilleries and quarries, some of which dated to the eighteenth century.[1]

The name "Powder Mill Branch," sometimes shown on early maps, can be explained by an 1813 newspaper ad that notes **Thomas Ewell** "has erected on the Potomac Canal about 3 miles from George Town a new and improved gun powder manufactory."[2] Three years later Ewell, was selling brass that was used in the powder mills, as well as distillery equipment. Originally announcing his intention to establish his operation at Stoddert's Mill in Bladensburg in 1811, he probably was

"Remains of Old Mill on the Potomac"
(Library of Congress)

influenced by the proximity of Foxall's Foundry located just west of Georgetown, which cast superior armaments.[3] The change in location was a fortuitous one, as the British would soon rout Americans at the Battle of Bladensburg and go on to burn and sack the Capital during the War of 1812.

83

Little Falls Branch

The waters of the Little Falls Branch were frequently touted as an excellent source of "fall" or waterpower. They were also hotly contested in disputes over water rights both when the C & O Canal was established at this location in 1832 and later, when the City of Washington's Receiving Reservoir was created.[4]

Upstream, the well-preserved private-property site of **Loughborough's Mill** can be seen from the adjacent Capital Crescent Trail in Little Falls Park, just above Massachusetts Avenue. The first mention of a mill here is in an 1831 tax assessment, which listed Nathan Luffborough (*sic*) as owner of a mill on 196 acres of "Friendship," with a value of $1,609.20. A census of 1850 described its principal product as corn meal, which was apparently used to feed slaves. The Loughboroughs were ardent southerners who fled to Virginia to fight for the Confederate cause. As a result, their nearby elegant stone home "Milton" was vandalized by Union soldiers stationed nearby, and their mill was ruined as well.[5]

John Eicholtz's painting, "Ruins of Loughborough Mill"
(Courtesy of the Historical Society of Washington, D.C.)

SLIGO CREEK

Although originally located in Prince George's County, **Sligo Mill** has been included in this guide as a result of an annexation to Montgomery County in recent years. The Sligo Creek watershed drains the areas southeast of Wheaton, Silver Spring and Takoma Park. The present-day community of Silver Spring was officially known as Sligo Post Office during the nineteenth century. The creek reportedly took its name from the famous Carroll family, who were from County Sligo, Ireland.

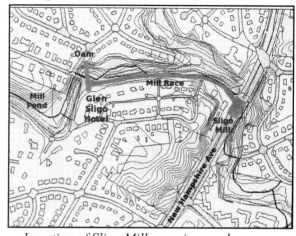

Location of Sligo Mill superimposed on map of Takoma Park
(Friends of Sligo Creek Park)

Sligo Mill's millrace can be seen running parallel to Sligo Creek in this undated photograph
(Friends of Sligo Creek Park)

An 1818 ad in the *National Messenger* newspaper listed Williams' and Carrolls' "extensive distillery and mill on Sligo . . . the improvements are a large brick distillery . . . and a well built mill adjoining it, all new and in complete order."[1]

According to a booklet produced for the 75th anniversary of Takoma Park,[2] real estate investor

85

Sligo Creek

Alva Wiswell built the Glen Sligo Hotel near the intersection of Elm and Heather Avenues. In addition, a rooftop pavilion was added to the foundation of the old mill. The *Washington Post* reported in 1899: "One of the exquisite bits of landscape architecture at Glen Sligo Pleasure Park is the Old Red Mill Roof Garden."[3] The structure was finally demolished in about 1920; the materials were used in nearby buildings. Although the site for the mill is now in Sligo Creek Park, no evidence of it remains.

Ruins of Sligo Mill
(Photograph courtesy of Arthur Colburn)

NOTES

Introduction
[1]*Maryland Gazette,* 1746

Background
[1]J. Thomas Scharf, *History of Western Maryland*, Vol. I, Philadelphia, 1892, pp. 645-647

Great Seneca Creek
[1]*Maryland Gazette,* February 9, 1769
[2]*Maryland Journal, and Baltimore Advertiser,* July 6, 1779
[3]Maryland State Archives Chancery Court #18 folio 476
[4]*Maryland Journal, and Baltimore Advertiser,* February 11, 1783
[5]Donald Jackson, editor, and Dorothy Twohig, associate editor, *Diary of George Washington,* 6 volumes, Charlottesville: University Press of Virginia, 1976-1979; Vol. IV, August 6, 1785, p. 176
[6]*Georgetown Centinel of Liberty,* April 19, 1799
[7]*Federal Republican and Commercial Gazette,* August 25, 1813
[8]*Dunlap's Pennsylvania Packet,* July 24, 1775
[9]Maryland State Archives Chancery Court Records, 1820s
[10]*Federal Republican and Commercial Gazette,* 1831
[11]*Frederick-Town Herald,* June 13, 1807
[12]Montgomery County, Maryland, Orphans' Court, March 13, 1813
[13]*Frederick-Town Herald,* December 21, 1816
[14]Montgomery County 1783 Tax Assessment
[15]Montgomery County Deeds, Liber E.B.P. 33 Folio 79
[16]*Portrait and Biographical Record,* 1898
[17]*Washington Federalist,* March 10, 1802
[18]*Maryland Journal and True American,* September 10, 1828
[19]*Georgetown Centinel of Liberty,* October 21, 1800 and *Frederick-Town Herald,* August 26, 1809; June 25, 1811
[20]Elsie White Haines, *Montgomery County Sentinel,* 1941

Little Seneca Creek and tributaries
[1]*Montgomery County Sentinel,* September 1895
[2]Montgomery County Road Plats, 1907
[3]*Frederick-Town Herald,* 1811

Little Seneca Creek and tributaries *(continued)*
[4]*Maryland Gazette*, July 13, 1775
[5]*Frederick-Town Herald*, 1799
[6]Report of Medley District Agricultural Society (MDAS), 1849

Rock Creek
[1]Montgomery County, 1783 Tax Assessment
[2]Montgomery County Deeds Liber I folio 345 and Liber V folio 74
[3]S. D. Caldwell, "Map of Bethesda District, Montgomery County, Maryland," *Directory*, 1915
[4]Interview with Col. E. Brooke Lee, 1972
[5]G. M. Hopkins, *Atlas of Montgomery County, Maryland, 1879*, Montgomery County Historical Society, 1975
[6]Interview with Bullard family, 1970s
[7]Road Petitions, 1880s
[8]Road Petitions, 1880s
[9]Montgomery County Deeds Liber A folio 574
[10]Montgomery County Deeds Liber 422 folio 107
[11]Maryland Journal Supplement (Baltimore), March 6, 1781
[12]Maryland State Archives Chancery Court Records, and *Georgetown Museum*, October 19, 1801
[13]*The Farmer's Friend*, October 1, 1840
[14]*Archaeological Investigations at the Horner's Mill Site*, Department of Anthropology, Montgomery College, Rockville, MD, 1975
[15]*Maryland Gazette*, November 17, 1772
[16]Clan Gregor Records
[17]*Maryland Journal, and Baltimore Advertiser*, April 3, 1787
[18]John J. Abert's 1838 Canal Map in U. S. Army Topographical Engineers "Report on Canal to Connect the Chesapeake and Ohio Canal with the city of Baltimore," Washington, D.C., 1838
[19]Montgomery County Deeds Liber JA 23 folio 223

Patuxent River
[1]*Maryland Journal, and Baltimore Advertiser*, June 22, 1787
[2]*Montgomery County Sentinel*, July 19, 1872
[3]G. M. Hopkins, *Atlas of Montgomery County, Maryland, 1879*, Montgomery County Historical Society, 1975

Patuxent River *(continued)*
[4]*Montgomery County Sentinel*, August 2, 1872; November 20, 1872
[5]*Maryland Journal, and Baltimore Advertiser,* October 10, 1780
[6]Thomas Canby and Elie Rogers, *Sandy Spring Legacy*, Sandy Spring Museum, 1999
[7]*Maryland Historical Magazine*, June 1948; *Washington Star* December 7, 1941
[8]*Maryland Journal, and Baltimore Advertiser*, 1775
[9]Montgomery County, 1783 Tax Assessment
[10]Abert, Martenet, Hopkins, *op.cit.*
[11]Interview with Harold W. Mullinix, Sr., 1972

Hawlings River
[1]*Maryland Gazette,* June 19, 1760; November 19, 1772
[2]Maryland State Archives Chancery Court Records, #18, 1789
[3]Annals of Sandy Spring, Sandy Spring Museum; Canby and Rogers, *op. cit.*
[4]Montgomery County Deeds Liber I Folio 376
[5]*Federal Republican and Commercial Gazette*, October 6, 1813
[6]Plat Courtesy of Sylvia Nash
[7]Mark Walston for Sugarloaf Regional Trails, 1977
[8]Interview with Speck family, 1975
[9]Montgomery County Deed Liber T 579

Paint Branch
[1]Montgomery County Tax Assessments. Montgomery County Deeds Liber JGH 3 folio 394; Liber JGH 9 folio 212; Liber EBP 24 folio 30
[2]Montgomery County Equity Court, Judgment Record Book, BS 3, folio 103
[3]Montgomery County Deeds Liber M folio 220
[4]Maryland State Archives Chancery Court Records, 1847
[5]*Frederick-Town Herald*, August 20, 1814
[6]Montgomery County Equity Court, Judgment Record Book, ES 2, Folio 367
[7]Montgomery County Equity Court Case #182
[8]Prince Georges County Unpatented Survey Certificate 337, Hall of Records, Annapolis, Maryland
[9]Michael F. Dwyer, "The Valley Mill on Paint Branch," *The Montgomery County Story*, Vol. 8, No. 1, February 1985
[10]Montgomery County Tax Assessments

Northwest Branch
[1] *Maryland Journal, and Baltimore Advertiser*, September 3, 1784
[2] Records of the Columbia Historical Society, Vol. 31 & 32
[3] Montgomery County, 1783 Tax Assessment. *Maryland Journal, and Baltimore Advertiser*, February 18, 1783. Maryland State Chancery Court Records, Liber ES 54 folio 196
[4] Records of the Columbia Historical Society, Vol. 31 & 32
[5] White House, June 21, 1904
[6] History of the Washington Suburban Sanitary Commission 75th Anniversary
[7] 1880 Plat, Montgomery County Historical Society
[8] *Montgomery County Sentinel*, July 19, 1902; February 4, 1919. Interview with Lecklider Family, 1982
[9] Montgomery County Deeds Liber BS Folio 494

Cabin John Creek
[1] Montgomery County, 1783 Tax Assessment. *GeorgeTown Weekly Ledger,* September 17, 1791
[2] *Maryland Gazette*, May 7, 1769
[3] Montgomery County Deeds Liber B, folio 242
[4] Montgomery County Deeds Liber N, folio 435
[5] *GeorgeTown Weekly Ledger,* September 9, 1791
[6] Biographical Dictionary of Congress, 1774-1961, p. 1254
[7] *Frederick-Town Herald*, November 10, 1804
[8] Michael F. Dwyer,"Magruder's Folly" *The Montgomery County Story*, Vol. 52, No. 3, Fall/Winter 2009
[9] Jane C. Sween, "All You Want to Know About the Magruders and a Little Bit More," unpublished manuscript, Sween Library, Montgomery County Historical Society
[10] "The Rambler," *Washington Star*, April 13, 1919
[11] Will of Samuel B. Magruder, Montgomery County Wills, 1818, Montgomery County Tax Assessment
[12] *Daily National Intelligencer.* (Washington City [D.C.]), July 12, 1849
[13] Note from Lily Stone, Montgomery County Historical Society. Communication from Irwin and Gloria Billick
[14] Montgomery County, 1837-1842 Tax Assessment
[15] *George-Town Centinel of Liberty*, March 28, 1800
[16] *George-Town Centinel of Liberty*, March 28, 1800

Watts Branch
[1] Peter Jefferson and Joshua Fry, *Map of Virginia, Maryland, and Delaware*, 1775
[2] Jackson and Twohig, *The Diaries of George Washington*, Vol. IV, 1785, op.cit.
[3] *Maryland Journal and True American*, November 24, 1830
[4] *Hopkins 1879 Atlas, op.cit.*
[5] Montgomery County, 1820 Tax Assessments
[6] *Maryland Journal and True American*, April 9, 1828
[7] *Maryland Journal and True American*, July 19, 1833
[8] Montgomery County Deeds Liber STS 3 folio 237
[9] 1850 Federal Census
[10] Portrait and Biographical Record, Sixth Congressional District, MD, Chapman Publishing Co., New York, 1898
[11] Interview with Veirs family, 1975
[12] J. Thomas Scharf, *History of Western Maryland, op. cit.*

Muddy Branch
[1] *Maryland Gazette*, November 7, 1782
[2] Montgomery County Land Records, 1813, lease agreement, Liber R, folio 13
[3] *Frederick-Town Herald*, October 7, 1815
[4] *Montgomery County Sentinel*, December 27, 1901
[5] *GeorgeTown Centinel of Liberty*, June 12, 1795
[6] Montgomery County, 1820 Tax Assessments
[7] *Frederick-Town Herald*, July 11, 1818
[8] Montgomery County Land Plat, John L. Dufief, 1878
[9] Charles Jacobs, Civil War Papers, Special Collection of Civil War Materials, Montgomery County Historical Society
[10] Katherine and Susan Aud, *Our Ancestors*, published by the authors, Silver Spring, MD, 1972, pg. 202

Bennett and Little Bennett Creeks
[1] Montgomery County, 1818 Tax Assessments
[2] *Frederick-Town Herald*, September 29, 1832
[3] The *Washington Post*, February 13, 1901
[4] Interview with the Gladhill family, 1989
[5] Mark Walston, *History of Hyattstown Mill*, interview with Ruth Mortimer Price, last Hyattstown miller, Washington, D.C.

Bennett and Little Bennett Creeks *(continued)*
[6]Mark Walston for Maryland-National Capital Park and Planning Commission
[7]Lynds A. Fralish, *Historic Mills of America*, Landmark Publishers, Inc., 1977
[8]Interview with Price Brown, 1992
[9]Interview with Leslie G. King, 1973

Little Monocacy River
[1]*Maryland Gazette*, May 7, 1772
[2]Maryland State Archives Chancery Court Records, 1790
[3]George Washington to Francis Deakens, July 1, 1794, in *George Washington Papers at the Library of Congress, 1741-1799, Series 2 Letterbooks,* p. 38
[4]*Frederick-Town Herald*, July 28, 1810
[5]*Washington Star*, December 8, 1935
[6]*Ibid.*
[7]Federal Census of Manufacturers
[8]1783 Tax Assessment
[9]*Frederick-Town Herald*
[10]T. H. S. Boyd, *History of Montgomery County, Maryland, 1879,* reprint by Heritage Books, Inc., Westminster, MD, 2008, p. 95
[11]Montgomery County Land Records, 1792
[12]Montgomery County Equity Court Records, 1822
[13]*Montgomery County Sentinel*, May 8, 1844
[14]Boyd, *op. cit.* p. 95
[15]Hopkins Atlas, *op. cit.*

Little Falls Branch
[1] Robert J. Kapsch, "The Potomac Canal: A Construction History," in *Canal History and Technology Proceedings*, Volume XXI, p.161
[2]*National Intelligencer,* 1811. *Federal Republican*, September 27, 1813
[3]Louis F. Gorr, "The Foxall Foundry: An Early Defense Contractor in Georgetown," in Records of the Columbia Historical Society, 1972

Little Falls Branch *(continued)*
[4]Bland's Reports, Maryland Chancery Court, 1809-1832, Case of Amos Binney
[5]James H. Johnson, *The Recollections of Margaret Cabell Brown Loughborough: A Southern Woman's Memories of Richmond, Virginia and Washington D.C. in the Civil War*, Lanham, MD, Hamilton Books, 2010, pp. 18, 93

Sligo Creek
[1]*National Messenger*, April 19, 1818
[2]Clifton E. Olmstead, *Takoma Park: A Photo History of its People by its People; 75 Years of Community living, 1882-1958*, Takoma Park, MD, 75th Anniversary Founders' Day Committee, 1958
[3]*Washington Post* Archives, 1899

Alphabetical Index to Mills

When a mill has had more than owner or operator, its most commonly recognized name is indicated by bold face in the text and in this index.

A - B
Alf Brown's Saw Mill, 36
Beall & Lackland's Union Mills, 70
Beall's Mill (Brooke Beall), 65
Beall's Mill (Walter Beall), 55
Beall's Old Mill, 65
Beckwith's grist and saw mill, 66
Bell's Mill, 62-64
Birdsall's Mill, 57
Black Rock Mill, 7, 13
Blair Mill, 23-24
Boone's Mill, 64
Bowie's Mill, 29
Brashear's grist and saw mill (Eli Brashear), 73
Brooke Beall's Mill, 65
Brooke Grove Mill, 38
Brooke's Mill (James Brooke), 37-38
Brookeville Woolen Factory, 39-41
Browningsville (mill at), 73
Brown's Saw Mill (Alf Brown), 36
Burnt Mills, 53-54

C
Cabbin John Mills, 60-61
Chandlee Mill, 38
Chaney's Mill, 53
Cloppers' Mill, 7, 14
Crows Mill, 16

D
Darby's Mill at Bucklodge, 20
Darby's Mill at Seneca, 12
Darby's Oakland Mill, 17
Davis Mill, 16-17
Dawson's Mill, 21
Doull's Mill, 60

D *(continued)*
Doyle's Mill, 36
Dydenhover's (Didenhover) fulling mill, 69
Dufeif's Mill, 70-72
Duvall's Mill, 36, 45, 50

E
Elgar's Mill, 8, 27
Eli Brashear's grist and saw mill, 73
Ellicott's Mill, 44
Eltinge's Mill, 11
Ewell's Powder Mill (Thomas Ewell), 83

F - G
Ford's Mill, 17
Foxall's Foundry, 83
Gaither's fulling mill, 36
Gaither's Mill, (W. B. Gaither), 41
Gamble's Mill (Mr. Gamble), 66
Gassaway's Mill, 13
Gladhill family mill, 74
Glen Mill, 65-67
Glenwood Mills, 70-71
Goshen Mill, 16-17
Gott's Mill, 77-78
Greenwood Mills, 40

H
Harper's Woolen Factory, 43
Haviland Mill, 34
Hipsley family mill, 39
Hipsley Mill Road, 36
Horner's Mill, 26
Hoyles Mill, 19-20
Hyattstown Mill, 74

95

J

James Brooke's Mill, 37-38
Jones Mill, 23

K

Kemp's Mill (on Northwest Branch), 49, 56-57
Kemps' Mill (on Paint Branch), 49
King's Distillery, 75
King's Grist and Sawmill, 76

L

Lansdale's Mill, 36
Lea-Haviland Mill, 34
Leawood Mills, 34
Little Paint Branch, the mill on, 50
Loughborough's Mill, 7, 84
Lukens' Mill, 46
Lyles' Mill, 79-81

M

Magruder's Folly, 61
Magruder's fulling mill (Samuel Wade Magruder), 60
Magruder's Mill (Samuel G. Magruder), 60
Magruder's Mill (Great Seneca), 17
Magruder's Mill (Cabin John Creek), 59
Major Hempstone's old brick mill, 79
McDade's old mill (Patrick McDade), 81
Mershbergers's Old Mill, 36
Middlebrook Mills, 15
Milford Mill, 21
Mill at Browningsville, 73
Mill on Little Paint Branch, 50
Millford Mills, 12
Morton's Mill, 78-79
Mount Carmel Mill Seat, 77
Mr. Gamble's Mill, 66
Mullinix Mill, 36
Muncaster's Mill, 6-8, 27-29
Musgrove's Old Mill, 41

N

Nathan White's Mill, 77
Needwood Mill, 26
Newlin's Mill, 39-40
Newport Mills, 24-25

O

O'Neal's Mill, 63
Oakland Mills (on the Monocacy), 78-79
Offutt's Watermill, 60
Old Newport Mills, 24-25
Old Red Mill, 86
Orndorff's Mill, 63
Owen's Mill, 29

P

Paint Branch Woolen Factory, 46
Patrick McDade's old mill, 81
Peck's Mills, 15
Perry's Old Mill, 67-68
Pierce Mill, 23
Pigman's Mill, 36
Pilling's Mill, 49-50
Plyer's Mill, 24
Powder Mill (Thomas Ewell's), 83
Price's Mills, 78
Pyle's Mill, 20

Q - R

Query Mill, 69
Rawlings Mill, 31, 34
Ray's former grist mill, 70
Ray's Mill, 24
Rev. Jimmie Day's Mill, 73
Richard Gott's Mill, 77-78
Ridgely's Mill, 31
Riggs Mill, 16
Robertson's Mill, 27-29
Rock Creek Mill, 25

S

Samuel B. Magruder's Mill, 62-63
Samuel Wade Magruder's fulling mill, 60
Seneca Mills, 12-13
Seneca Stone Mill, 7, 12
Sligo Mill, 85-86
Snowden's Mill, 48
Stoddert's Mill, 83

T

Thomas' Mill, 39
Triadelphia, 34
Tschiffely Mill, 12
Turner's Mill (William Turner), 73

V

Valley Mill, 7, 49-51
Veirs Mill, 25
Viers Saw Mill, 20

W

W. B. Gaither's Mill, 41
W. Williams Mill, 81
Walker's Mill, 16
Walter Beall's Mill, 43
Ward's Mill, 81
Waters Mill, 19
Watkins Mill, 15-16
Webster's Mill, 77
Weer family mill, 39
Wheatley family mill, 24
Wheeler's Mill, 69
White's Mill (Zachariah White), 59
White's new mill on Little Monocacy
    (Zachariah White), 77
William Turners Mill, 72
Williams and Carrolls distillery and mill, 85
Williams' Mill (W. Williams), 81
Wilson's Sawmill, 75
Wooton's Mill, 67

Y - Z

Young's Mill, 21
Zachariah White's Mill, 51
Zachariah White's new mill on Little
    Monocacy, 77
Zeigler's Bone and Sawmill, 74

97